JOURNEY TO A
SIX-FIGURE
INCOME:
THE BLUEPRINT

NETWORK MARKETING MASTERY:
LESSONS FROM LEADERS

JOURNEY TO A
SIX-FIGURE
INCOME:
THE BLUEPRINT

NETWORK MARKETING MASTERY:
LESSONS FROM LEADERS

TGON Publishing

TGON Publishing

Warning—Disclaimer

The purpose of this book is to educate and inspire. This book is not intended to give advice or make promises or guarantees that anyone following the ideas, tips, suggestions, techniques or strategies will have the same results as the people listed throughout the stories contained herein. The author, publisher and distributor(s) shall have neither liability nor responsibility to anyone with respect to any loss or damage caused, or alleged to be caused, directly or indirectly by the information contained in this book.

CONTENTS

"An investment in knowledge pays the best interest."

— Benjamin Franklin

INTRODUCTION

Have you ever hesitated to take a leap because you felt you weren`t ready? Or perhaps you held back from sharing your knowledge or ideas, thinking that there were others more qualified than you? I`m confident that all of us have felt this way at least once.

Recently I took up pickleball. It`s a fun sport that has gotten me excited about competing again on the court. After years of playing tennis competitively in high school and college, it felt great to be on the court again. The only problem; I felt like I wasn`t ready to play in the "big leagues" and enter a tournament in the 5.0 category. Funny thing how sometimes our own mindset holds us back. Just last week, I decided to get over myself and enter a tournament in the 5.0 category. I told myself that even if I didn`t win, there were lessons and experiences that I could only have at this rank. To my joy and amazement, I found this to be true! I loved playing against opponents that were challenging and working on my own technique. It also didn`t hurt that I ended up winning the entire thing!

In network marketing, as in life, (or even pickleball), that mindset that holds us back from going all in is very common. Have you heard the story of the canoe team? It is one of my favorites! The story of the Hawaiian canoe team embodies what it truly means to defy expectations and believe in oneself. The canoeist who dared to propose a new challenging route faced discouragement and ridicule, yet a few decided to join him. The triumph they experienced upon reaching their destination was the reward of their courage and determination.

Much like the brave canoeist and his team, many network marketers face similar challenges. They face skepticism and even ridicule from others, they are afraid of the judgments and assessments of others, and sometimes, they even hesitate to embark on this entrepreneurial journey. Yet, there are those who dare to dream bigger, to see beyond the horizon. These are driven by their desire for financial independence, a better lifestyle, or new experiences. They have the courage to ask, "Why not me?"

As a network marketing coach, author, and speaker, I, can attest that fear of judgment is one of the biggest barriers network marketers face. Yet, your uniqueness, your perspective, and your experiences are precisely what makes you valuable in this field. I`ve grown several successful businesses over decades in network marketing and always emphasize the importance of personal development. The company, the product, and the people are all elements of the equation. But the most critical variable is you.

In this extraordinary book, my co-authors and I share our collective wisdom gleaned from years of successful network marketing. Each of these wonderful individuals took part in a unique mastermind in Oceanside, California, each one penned their own chapter, and each shared their unique perspective on network marketing.

As you delve into these pages, you`ll find a kaleidoscope of experiences, insights, and strategies. From people who have battled fear and doubt, persevered through the darkest times, and emerged victorious, building their own network marketing businesses from the ground up. I assure you their chapters are invaluable to newcomers and veterans in the industry alike.

Each chapter is presented by a different author, providing a brief bio, their accomplishments, and favorite quotes. My personal "Coach`s notes" are sprinkled throughout the book, sharing additional insights and thoughts. I recommend having a notepad ready, as each chapter contains actionable steps to help you succeed in your own network marketing journey.

Connect with these authors on social media and share your thoughts about their chapters. Your interaction and feedback is appreciated.

Lastly, I want to express my gratitude. I am honored and humbled to serve the network marketing industry and to have the opportunity to coach thousands of inspiring individuals. My work has taken me around the globe, and I`m always amazed by the incredible people I meet. Thank you for trusting me as your coach, and I look forward to our continued journey together.

Ready to embark on this journey? Open the first chapter, and let`s get started!

"God can handle your doubt, anger, fear, grief, confusion, and questions. You can bring everything to him in prayer."

— Rick Warren

ANGELO TANDANG AND KRISTINE JOHANN TINGCANG

- Building a business together while also being able to travel.

- Helping empower people worldwide, especially in the Philippines.

- Became successful through small wins every day and now teaching you to do the same!

The Art of Self-Marketing

Sell a product – you can earn a couple of bucks.

Sell yourself – you can earn a fortune.

In multi-level marketing, it doesn`t really matter what company you are in or what products you offer because there are a lot of network marketers with the same company as you, and even tons of MLM companies, whether it`s big or small with high successful network marketers selling the same products as you. Even if you have the advantage of having the latest and cutting-edge technology for your products, it doesn't guarantee that the distributor will be 100% successful.

Likewise, some companies have just common or mid-range quality products in the market but still create millionaires along the way. Why is that so? Ultimately, you only sell yourself and your vision. That's why you should know that in this business, you need to master the art of self-marketing.

I often hear this phrase, "People don't buy the company or products; people buy people."

Coach's Notes: Kylie Jenner pulls out a lipstick, and people buy it. Michael Jordan brings out a new sneaker, and people buy it. Steve Jobs launches a new Apple, and people buy it. Taylor Swift releases a new album, and people buy it. The authors here have drawn a brilliant parallel, emphasizing the importance of personal branding and influence. Remember that being famous is only one part of branding in these examples. Angelo and Kristine are going to teach you the other parts!

It's evident that people adore other people, especially celebrities, athletes, businessmen, superstars and the like. Once these high-profile people share or sell a product or service, they tend to buy it even though they are not experts or creators.

Kylie Jenner pulls out a lipstick, and people buy it.

Michael Jordan brings out a new sneaker, and people buy it.

Steve Jobs launches a new Apple, and people buy it.

Taylor Swift releases a new album, and people buy it.

Heart Evangelista is a famous social media fashion influencer. She once painted an abstract and sold it for $60,000. She also added in an interview that if ever her artwork is sold at NFT digital art, its price may go as high as $3,000,000.

Other artists are way more talented and paint better than her, but they can't sell their artwork like hers. People don't just buy the painting; they buy the person.

You may see this as a disadvantage. Maybe you just started in your life; you are young, not much of a talented person, and the fact that most of the people you know -your family; relatives, and friends they do buy only from people who have big names, like athletes, actors/ actresses, and influencers. Moreover, they might also care less about whatever you are sharing. But if you look closely, you really have a big advantage here.

Since you know this hack already that people buy from a person who has a big influence, you don't just say, "I can't be successful in this business because no one buys from me, I'm just a small business owner".

Say, "How can I be a person of influence?"

"How do I position myself in such a way that people look up to me as an influencer?"

The good news is you can be an influencer. You will position yourself as a person of value. You will have your own name. People will see you as the brand. And when you sell something, people will buy it, not because of the product, but because it's you.

Don't limit yourself to who you are now and how people know you.

You can start rebranding yourself as big as you can imagine you could be.

You can reset your mind and bring out the best version of yourself - a self-made superstar/millionaire.

People don`t like the feeling of being sold, but they like to buy.

One of the most common challenges of a network marketer is how to get people to reply to them when they message. People don`t like to engage with them because they sound salesy. All they do is market their product or service. Making it seem like all the problems in the world can be solved by their product.

I remember what our mentor told us, "If Mark Zuckerberg or Jeff Bezos messaged you, would you reply?". Definitely – a big Yes! A huge opportunity is coming in.

That is the power of making a name for yourself. If you can consistently show up and be known for adding value, people will want to talk with you.

Coach's Notes: Angelo and Kristine's insights are particularly interesting here. Consider your online presence. What would a visitor to your social media profile think of you? Would they see someone who offers value and has influence? This is why it's important to curate your online image carefully.

People are judgemental. That is just how it is. Once you have met someone, they immediately go to your profile and judge you based on a few swipes. If they see nothing valuable, nothing interesting, and worst, a profile that posts only something that he sells, nobody will ever reply back to you.

But if you always share entertaining, valuable, inspiring, and relatable content, then you message someone, I bet they`ll be excited to reply!

"Ohh, this person is so inspiring I always see his content I wonder what he`s up to right now?"

When I message people, most of them reply because they see me as a person of influence and value. This also creates a positive impression and curiosity "Why, of all the people who follow him on social media, was I messaged?"

When you start setting yourself up in public, people buy your authenticity and your relatability.

Instant fame and success can kill your marketing. People can immediately feel that it`s not you, it isn`t real, or you`re just boasting around, or worse, you can be unfriended/blocked. While there is no substitute for hard work, doing random self-marketing or posting can only do so much. You must also apply the Pareto principle or 80/20 rule to be effective. It literally means 80% of the result comes from 20% of work.

Why has Social Media Made it Easy?

Social media is now proof that you exist. It`s a catalyst for reaching a bigger audience. You may know some successful network marketers before that didn`t have social media profiles, they just had phone contacts/emails/telemarketing/family and friend referrals, but nowadays, people are smart. They search a lot, are more skeptical than ever and don`t even want to be bothered at all. So how can we reach out and connect to them?

Social media is a tool that we can take advantage of. It`s also a platform that can magnify the person you want to be if you do it well. Consequently, if you do it poorly, it can also escalate a bad impression from your audience. So, you must be clear about your intentions in creating an impact.

First, you must consider how to stand out from the crowd. Do not overthink; spend all your time figuring out what content will hit big! Just do it! The one thing that will set you up in the crowd is showing up daily. Keep posting even if the photos are not good. Intentionally post not-good photos so you can have a story to tell and look back on the changes. You might lose your relatability and authenticity if you always post good stuff. You don`t need to be someone else. Just be yourself.

Do the Unusual

Our company rewarded us with a travel incentive to Bali, Indonesia. The culture, the famous gates, the food, and the people made our travel incentive memorable. While other associates are just taking photos and videos. We were already doing Facebook live videos, sharing our thoughts, giving value, sharing how grateful we are, and the journey of how we came to travel. It creates an impression that "it`s real, real-time because it`s live; it can`t be edited."

After that trip, people were curious about what we do for a living. If you also want to save future posts on certain travels, you can have plenty of dresses/shirts/clothes to wear in a day. People are now messaging me, asking what my business is, and that`s what you really want, to make them curious and to make them ask. Whenever you can, do live videos on weekdays. While other people are in their office, stressed at work, you are showing them an option. Knowing the wrong things to avoid is just as important as knowing the right things to do.

Quality or Quantity or Both?

It`s not quality vs quantity. It is quantity done over time, working out for you so you can have eventual quality. Remember, everything in this business is a numbers game. Just like a habit, you can also build a muscle in creating content and posting to social media so that the time will come self-marketing is no longer a work that requires a lot of brain cells because it`s already a habit. These habits create a ratio of shots that you can easily identify what`s nice from not. It is also good to watch some basic photography to grasp ideas and minimize bad photos.

On our Bali incentive trip, we took over four thousand pictures. We didn`t know yet which were quality or not. We just took as many pictures as possible because we cannot repeat the event. We can only take so many pictures. We also prepared twelve outfits for a four-day three-night trip, meaning we had four different outfits daily. I cannot say that those we`ve handpicked to be posted only were the quality ones already. But I can say we`re posted a ton of good photos spread out over days to maximize a month`s worth of content to inspire people from our incentive trips and to share with them it is possible.

Create a Calendar

Do not fall into the trap of your emotions. Posting negative energy when you are low, posting hype-upped energy when you are high. Create a weekly calendar and a monthly calendar. Stick to it, whatever happens. Here is also the reality, even though we don`t plan ahead of time, our calendars, months, and days fill themselves up, whether bad or good or both. We can be wiser to do the necessary things and speed up our MLM Business.

Accountability Partner

When we work out our social media marketing, it`s best to have someone who checks on you and has an accountability partner. There`s a built-up of positive relationships, whether mutual or friendly competition. A good example is that your accountability partner can take photos of you and remind you to be consistent on social media. It`s an advantage to have quality photos of you with someone versus a selfie. Treat your tools as an investment in creating your social media. We started with an Android phone that was just $300, and months later. We upgraded to an Apple phone with high storage ranging a price of $1,700; again, a few months later, we studied and added a drone to our self-marketing worth $1,100. As your money grows, be accountable for reinvesting the tools that widen your market reach.

What Monkey see, Monkey do

If all you do today is seen and duplicated by your downline, will you be happy about the result? Downlines copy you, whether it`s good or bad. I did my first ever Facebook live video in January 2022. I was so scared! I might say the wrong words, I might look dumb. I was at the beach then; I might also lose the connection while doing the live video, but I did it anyway. Of course, as it turned out, I wasn`t harmed doing the live video, but it is not that good! Add to it the quality of the video because I was only using an Android phone that costs $300. I only had 200 views. But I was so happy that I finally did my first Facebook Live.

I recruited a board exam top-notcher to my team in February 2022. Since he already saw me consistently posting content and doing Facebook Live, I didn`t have a hard time convincing him that he should also post content and do Facebook Lives. When he did his first ever Facebook live, he had 1,200 views! That`s 600% more than my reach. Imagine if all your associates do the same thing and create a bigger audience reach; how big of an organization you`ll have?

You will have momentum and will set a team culture that always shows up on social media. Soon enough, you`ll be seeing the compound effect of your simple post, simple reel, and simply live. All because you set the example that anyone can give value to social media without worrying about being seen as perfect, just being real.

Self-marketing is like icing on a cake. Your company is the store. We attract prospects based on the cake presentation. Increasing the likeliness of the icing attracts more customers to take a look at what we can offer. You can also attract different types of prospects based on the relatability, authenticity, and value you share. Below you will find my observation from posting over a year`s time.

IF YOU POST:

1 Day – It just says you exist on social media platforms.

1 Week – This creates highlights about you and impressions from other people.

1 Month – You gave an introduction of your background and can create interest from other people.

3 Months – Some people will follow your habits and generate your social brand/what to buy from you.

6 Months – If you look back from where you started, it`s like the season from planting, then less friction in connecting with cold markets and then harvesting your efforts.

1 YEAR – It creates a social proof of you, and you can now evaluate and create a better style

A YEAR or So – You become more creative about what you are posting, and you feel it`s much easier and fun.

Self-marketing takes time, and so is your skills and growth in business. Be patient because you can never see the growth in just one post. There will be a time you are going to feel anxious of what you are doing, just keep posting every single day, and trust the process by letting the compound effects work in your favor.

Coach's Notes: The authors have rightly emphasized the importance of consistency in this industry. It's not a one-time affair but a continuous effort to provide value and solidify your position as an influencer. Seeing the authors' dedication and how they have used their personal brand to become a successful network marketer is inspiring.

As you master the art of self-marketing, you yourself can create unlimited prospects to invite. You will no longer be afraid of how and where to start. Fear will always be there, but because of the confidence in your daily habits, you will be bold, and braveness will give you direction. The consistency you established will help your team and downlines understand that it`s just part of the process of simplifying things in creating leads.

"What you do today can improve all of your tomorrows."

– Ralph Marston

"What you do today determines all of your tomorrows."

– My spin-off of this quote

CHEYENNE GLADE WILSON

- Had never done network marketing before and lived in the poorest place per capita in the entire USA - Pine Ridge Reservation, South Dakota.

- Earned auto bonus in twenty three days and reached the top rank of her company in six months.

- Earned a million dollars in commissions in three years and three months (Millionaire Award Recipient).

- VIP Auto Elite Bonus earner for the past five years (since it launched).

- Top twelve in the company with the most personally enrolled customers on auto-ship, and top twelve for most customers who receive their products free through a referral program.

Pushing 'Past'ure Limits

I`m proud to be a fifth-generation rancher. I grew up in the middle of nowhere in the Big Sky Country of Montana. Things are quite vast out here, and responsibilities quickly find their way to the young. I treasure all that I have learned along the way. From a young age, I learned about leadership from things I experienced first-hand. Animals have always been a big part of my life. They have taught me a lot over the years. For this reason, I use a lot of analogies that involve livestock. I hope you can follow along with me as I explain a little bit about self-limiting beliefs.

Coach's Notes: Cheyenne beautifully blends personal experiences with deep insights into human behavior. The analogy of livestock and their behavior makes her message relatable and unique to her own story. Her ability to draw wisdom from her environment makes her insights valuable and applicable to anyone.

A pasture is what keeps our cattle from roaming around. Different pastures are used to rotate cattle`s eating patterns and keep them on their owner`s land. Cattle respect the wire barrier for the most part. They know there is little give if they lean against the fence, so they are content with staying in the pasture. However occasionally a fence-crawler, a cow pushing against the fence to break out, comes along and disturbs the peace. Once a cow gets out of the pasture, it is hard to get her back inside the wire barrier, and it`s even harder to keep her in the pasture that she escaped from.

I have a lot of experience observing these freedom-seekers. After dealing with them for quite a few years, their behavior put my thoughts into overdrive. Why did they want out? What was wrong with the pasture they were in? What was so enticing about the other side of the fence? Why didn`t they want to stay in once they were put back in the original pasture? What drove them to rebel against the barrier of the pasture? Did they have their own thoughts, drive, and desire to get out? Why did this appeal to me?

We all know people who are stuck in their lives. They are bored, complacent, and don`t really push past their own barriers. I believe these folks are like the cattle in the pasture that never try to find a way through the fence.

There are also people out there who are driven, focused, and goal-oriented. I call these types of people "mavericks." A maverick is an unbranded bovine that is running free. I don`t know about you, but something about that is appealing to me. I know I`m talking about cattle here, but I never want to be a sheep. I don`t want to live the same day over and over for eighty years and try to call that a life. I want to push past my limits, find a way through the barriers, and achieve all my goals. I want to push myself, I want to fail forward, and I want to be proud of all I accomplish. How about you?

I believe there is a reason that once a cow finds its way through the fence, it doesn`t want to stop crawling through. It is a choice. Once that taste of freedom sets in, nothing else comes close. I believe our mindset is this way, also. Once you discover the power of staving off negativity, the mere existence of it almost brings on nausea.

In order to change something, you must identify what you want to change. Simply saying you want to change your mindset is too vague. You must break it down into bite-sized lumps. This makes it so much easier to focus on each step that must be taken in order to change that behavior completely.

What self-limiting belief do you want to change right now?

Coach's Notes: Cheyenne makes a profound point about the importance of specificity when aiming for change. Vague desires often lead to half-hearted attempts and inconclusive outcomes. The clarity she encourages is the first step toward effective transformation.

Think hard about this question. The answer shouldn't come to you right away. The thoughts that come to you right away are going to be too vague. I'll use an example of my own...

For years, I wanted to lose weight. When I say years, I should say decades. I've battled my weight for over thirty years. My ultimate goal was to lose weight, get healthy, and be happy. Sounds simple, right? Well, it's not. Over the past thirty years, I have tried just about every diet, get-thin-quick schemes, etc. I have lost plenty of weight but also gained it right back. On top of that, I usually gained back more, so I was heavier after the weight loss attempt than I was before I started. This created a vicious cycle of defeat.

The past couple of years brought me to a new low. I'm sure the pandemic had something to do with it, and I know I'm not the only one that has struggled. However, blaming my situation was not helped by blaming it on the pandemic. I realized when I did that I was giving my power away.

I decided to really examine the root of why I had food issues and when they began. I discovered a whole slew of things that I never expected. I went through the lowest and loneliest time of my life. My business and personal life suffered. However, somehow through it all, I knew I had to go through it if I was ever going to make a meaningful and lasting change. After some major soul-searching, I realized that something traumatic had happened to me when I was seven years old. It just came to me one day out of the blue.

I almost thought I had dreamt it, but something deep inside me knew that the truth had finally surfaced. As I analyzed this new knowledge, I realized that I began to use food for comfort at that time in my life. I finally knew that my eating disorder began so long ago.

Coach's Notes: Cheyenne's journey toward understanding the root cause of her issues demonstrates her courage and tenacity. It's inspiring to see how she confronted her past, faced her traumas, and used this self-knowledge as a catalyst for positive change.

Once I had this knowledge, I had to figure out what to do with it. I had become a certified health coach a few years earlier, so I was equipped with what to do. I began by dissecting the information that came to light. I allowed all the self-limiting beliefs that I had about myself to surface. I was able to see right through them all. I understood right away that most of my self-limiting beliefs were lies.

I also realized that those beliefs were instilled in me by someone else in my life. Once I acquired this knowledge, it became a lot easier to let those beliefs go, and I was able to forgive myself. Forgive myself? Yes, forgive myself. So many of our limiting beliefs also have guilt associated with them. It was time to make peace with myself and to give myself some grace.

That is exactly what I did. I allowed myself to grieve for the little girl I never got to be. I allowed myself time to be pissed off. I allowed myself time to cry. I allowed myself time to exist with no judgment. I came through it all, and on the other side, I emerged as a completely new person. I viewed my weight as something connected to my health. I was able to create a new plan of living for myself. I followed through with it, and each day was exciting.

There was no negativity. I was kind to myself and gave myself time to figure it out. I was able to identify what I truly wanted and the dynamics of the steps that it would take me to get there. I believed in, and pushed myself.

I write this now seventy pounds lighter than I was seven months before I started this journey. I have gone on to help others duplicate my results. For the first time in my life, I am helping others with so much hope and gratitude. I know what it`s like to struggle and not feel worthy. Helping others discover their worth and personal power fills my cup.

This new fire in my belly isn`t just centered on the physical side of my life. It embodies everything in my life. I believe that one area affects all others. If something is off in a big way (or even in a small way), it can have detrimental consequences in other areas. I struggled for years in my private life and in my business because of my weight. Crazy, huh?! It wasn`t just about my weight...it was about everything. My weight was just the outward display of what was going on in my soul. Once I gave myself time and grace, I fixed not only the one thing I wanted to but also so much more than I intended to.

Coach's Notes: The transformation that Cheyenne has undergone is truly commendable. It's a great example of how personal breakthroughs can lead to becoming a source of inspiration and help for others. The interconnectedness she points out between various aspects of life is an important insight that we all can learn from. She truly embodies the idea that change is not just about one aspect of life; it's about overhauling your entire mindset and lifestyle.

All of this happened because I got tired of being in the same pasture. I wasn`t afraid to try to escape. I pushed myself past my limits and discovered so much more along the way. If I can do this, so can you. I have a feeling that the one thing you want to change about yourself is masking something else. I`m not a psychologist, but I have found this true in almost every person I have encountered. It`s not a bad thing. It`s a huge area of opportunity if you look at it right.

The questions you will want to ask yourself on your path to meaningful change are:

Am I happy?
Do I want more?
Do I feel free?
Am I fulfilled?
Do I live?
Do I love?
Do I matter?

Once you know the answers to those questions, you will know what you need to do next. Learning to push past your self-limiting beliefs is something that you get better at through practice. One thing will turn into another thing. You will invite the challenge. You will no longer see change as a scary thing and feel like you can`t do it. You WILL do it, and you will be smiling big as you look back on your progress.

I wish that for you! If you need help finding yourself, I know a place in Montana that will put you close to Mother Nature. Sometimes when too much noise is going on in your head, it`s hard to think. Slow down. Shut out the noise. If those things fail, feel free to come for a self-seeking adventure. I`ve got lots of pastures out here. Let`s break through those barriers together!

"It always seems impossible until it's done."

— Nelson Mandela

JENNIE JO

- Six figure earner.

- Number one promoter of the year in all of North America.

- Co-Author of this best seller.

- Launched my own company.

My name is Jennie Jo, and I am a full-time single mama to three littles ones, all under the age of eight. When I say full-time, I mean it! My kids are with me 24/7. With no family, no friends, and no daycare, I like to say that I constantly have three shadows with me all of the time. That may seem overwhelming for some, but I feel incredibly blessed that I get to have them by my side as I create this life. I also homeschool and just launched my own company. Sometimes, things may be busy and chaotic, but I wouldn`t trade this life for anything.

Of course, it wasn`t always like that. I had to start over from nothing. I got myself and my kids out of a very toxic environment. I felt like I had my back up against the wall, and it was challenging to be brave enough to have my own back and leave. But I did! And I am so grateful for that.

Coach's Notes: Jennie Jo's story of escaping a toxic environment and starting from scratch is truly remarkable. As a coach, I want to emphasize her determination and bravery. Her journey serves as an inspiration to anyone facing challenges in life. Everyone can learn from her example that they can overcome obstacles and succeed in network marketing with the right mindset and a desire to change.

If you had come across my social media a couple of years ago, you would have noticed a few things. First, I probably had about sixty-eight Facebook friends. Seriously. It was bad. I also didn`t post that much. I am an introvert who struggled to connect and, most of the time didn`t like other people. The thought of posting about my life and interacting with people online terrified me and honestly, was not my jam.

When I left the toxic relationship, I realized very fast that I needed to figure out how to make money while still being with my babies. For any other women out there, you know how stressful this HUGE obstacle can be. Lucky for me, and for you...we have both found our way to network marketing. Network marketing and specifically, social media were the key for me to make this happen for me and my kids.

In this chapter, I want to share how I went from having sixty eight friends to having half a MILLION friends across multiple social platforms. I will share with you how you can start where you are right now and create a social selling platform that helps you provide for yourself and yours. I will also share how I started from scratch, and you can too.

One of the first things you need to be successful in this industry isn't what you probably think it is. You don't need a huge following; you don't need to know your product or service the best. The very first thing you need when starting network marketing is a desire to make changes in your life. You have to have a desire to take ownership of your time and what you are doing. If you have the DESIRE, you can make incredible things happen.

Social platforms may feel overwhelming, but I promise that these can be really great FREE tools that can help you grow a business. Most people haven't realized how much leverage you have by using social platforms to grow, so in this chapter, I will teach you how to take advantage of them.

Think back to before the internet existed. If you had a business, the majority of your business would have been done locally. Now with the internet and social platforms, you literally have access to billions of people.

We all know the "old way" of doing network marketing. Make a list of people you know, go and talk to them, and make an offer. This is a tried and true method, and I still think you should do it. The only problem is that your list is going to run out eventually. So, how do you keep the list going and continue to meet new people? That is where social platforms and video come into play.

Attraction marketing means creating engaging content that attracts people to consume what we are making. It doesn't matter if it is a post about the product or a funny video featuring you and the humor of motherhood. Attraction marketing is anytime you put something out there that people can consume.

Let's go back to me, pre-network marketing. Social media wasn't my jam, and I sure wasn't going to spend my time creating content of myself to let people I know watch. But my DESIRE to provide for myself and my babies was high. I had a drive to succeed. I had no excuses. I had to make this work. So, when I found out about attraction marketing and using video to attract new people to you, I jumped at the chance to make it work.

The second thing you need to be successful is DRIVE. Desire is great, and it helps us believe that this may be possible for us. But DRIVE is what gets us into action. It helps a single introverted mom decide she can put herself out there on social platforms. It`s what helps us figure out what is going to work for us.

When I started with the short-form videos, Facebook reels weren`t even a thing yet. So, I tiptoed my way into the Tik Tok pool, and somehow things blew up. I started with doing trends, then realized there was power in storytelling. Well, that`s when the powers above intervened, and I got kicked out of my Tik Tok account! With nowhere else to go, I wondered what was next. Failure is never an option for me, nor is quitting. Just then, Facebook reels opened up. It felt like it was the right platform, with the right tool that I liked using.

I just started repurposing the old Tik Tok videos that I had saved, and they started going viral on Facebook reels. Reel after reel started having amazing views, and I was blown away. How could a single mom with sixty eight followers all of a sudden have millions of views on her reels?!

That`s the power of social platforms. I gave myself the time and space to figure out how to do it, and then I started to authentically share about my life in ways that felt fun to me. It wasn`t and still isn`t all about the product and company. It`s about letting people see who I am.

If you are new to social platforms OR have never posted a video, remember that it`s ok to start small. Your job isn`t to do five videos a day, and you are absolutely NOT supposed to be an expert at this. Your job is to post at least one video a day consistently. It can be about anything. Talk about your kids being in school or your favorite summer vacation. Share about what distracts you from your work or how you met your spouse. It doesn't matter what it is. You just have to realize that consistency wins! Every single time.

Coach's Notes: Jennie Jo's success on social platforms highlights the importance of being consistent and authentic. As a coach, I encourage readers to embrace her approach of consistently posting content that reflects their genuine interests. Authenticity builds trust with the audience, making it easier to attract potential customers. By staying true to themselves and their passions, they can create a loyal following and stand out in the competitive world of social selling.

Now, some of you are already well-versed in social platforms. If this is you, I want to encourage you to set up a posting schedule for yourself. Think about mixing it up with short-form videos and static posts. This helps people stay engaged, and the social platforms love it!

The next thing is that you should be consistent with your content. For example, pick five things that you want to post about. I encourage people to do this because all of us are multipurpose people! We all love different types of things, but it can be confusing and a jumbled mess if you post about all your hobbies and interests all the time. Five is a great number of interests and topics that keep people engaged.

So pick your five things to post about and then stay consistent with it. If I decide to post about being a single mom, that would be one of my topics. I am going to connect with other single moms starting over from scratch, so I can share a checklist of things I wish I had done before I left OR a little background and some of my story. Our content should be about connecting with others and helping them solve a pain point in their lives. Be intentional about what content you are putting out.

Side note here, but it is super important. Please choose five areas that you are actually interested in. Someone once said they wanted to talk to single moms, and I asked, "Are you a single parent?" They said, "Well, no, but I think it is a great target audience." Choosing topics you are interested in is more beneficial than choosing topics you THINK people want to hear about. If you love Disney, talk about Disney! If you have a passion for Lego, create content around it. You will be more successful talking about content you care about than about something you think will help sell your product. Talk to people like you. Those are the easiest people to talk to!

Now, we have gone over how to become consistent, whether you are starting from scratch or if you are a seasoned pro. You should stay consistent with the topics you are posting about and it should be a mixture of static posts and videos. The next thing to remember is that you want to mix up your topics.

I`m going to share with you something I wish I had been taught years ago. Don`t try and fix something that isn`t broken! If you get engagement on your posts and videos, just keep doing what you do! If you find yourself losing the engagement, that is the time to play around with things and tweak your strategy. Don`t throw it all out just because it isn`t working right now.

I have given you a couple of tools and strategies that you can start today. I encourage you to start today. Don`t wait and tell yourself that you need more training, more content, more anything. You are ready! But I do want to address the big 'ol elephant in the room. As easy as this sounds, it can be challenging to do.

When I first started posting on social media, it was a challenge. It wasn't my personality to put my face out there. I didn't want people I knew to see me and judge me. Every single day when I woke up, I would think to myself, "I don't want to post today." People can be mean. People will try and tear you down. But I want to remind you that your desire and drive need to push you to do hard things. If you have kids that are relying on you, you owe it to them and, more importantly, to YOURSELF to not give into your own excuses. Every time I feel mine creeping back in, I look at my kids and see the most powerful three reasons to do it anyways.

Once you are consistent, have some topics you like, and are mixing it up with static posts and videos, it's time to work on your storytelling. All of us are storytellers. We call our best friend and tell her about the crazy guy at the gym today, tell each other about how our day was, and tell our kids stories about what it was like when we were growing up. We are made to connect through stories. So, it is only natural that some of the best content we will create will be around telling a story. So I made a couple of reels telling my story. Those reels hit 25 million views on Facebook! That is what happens when we share our stories. So if I can encourage you to do one thing, it's to get good at telling stories! Record yourself telling a story, and then watch it back. What needs to be cleaned up? What do you need to take out? Where can you use tone to get people engaged?

You have posted, are consistent, and use stories to connect more deeply with people. You may think your work is done, but it's only just begun! Like Rob always says, the fortune is in the follow-up, which goes for selling on social platforms.

When you start to get traction with social posts, you are going to have people commenting on your posts. They may even start to DM you. This is all good news because it helps engagement. This is also an opportunity for you to engage with people personally. Don`t ever take advantage of that! You gain a huge trust factor when you engage with people`s comments.

Once you start engaging with people in the comments, you can jump over to Messenger, and they are much more likely to engage with you there if you have been commenting back to them from your post.

Messenger is amazing because you can directly converse with people here. You can ask them questions and figure out what they are personally struggling with. I personally love sending people a voice recording in Messenger. It is such a surprise for people; they love having one more level of connection with me. It also helps them know they are interacting with you, not your VA or a copy/paste situation. People feel valued when you take the time to connect to them personally.

When making an offer in Messenger, the best thing you can do is make their next step EASY. If you have another thirty links and forms for someone to go through, the likelihood that they will do it is very slim. Make it easy to buy from you! What would be the easiest way for someone to get started with me and then figure out if your company or upline already has something in place, or figure it out? I love the example of selling things on Instagram. Right now, someone can see an ad and click on a link. It takes them directly to the page to buy, and the consumer is STILL on Instagram. They figured out how to make it so easy to purchase through the app. When you are making an offer through Messenger, help it be easy for your new person.

In closing, there are a couple of questions I want to answer that I always get asked when I am presenting this topic at retreats and events.

What is the best social platform to be on?

Any platform will work! My main thing is that you have to like to engage in it. If you hate Tik Tok, don`t try and build on Tik Tok.

Facebook is still my predominant lead, for sure. It is a killer platform for creating content, communicating with my team, and building a loyal following. But you can do that on many different platforms. Facebook is my jam and the king in my world, but do what works for you.

How can I get more engagement?

This sounds crazy that I need to mention this, but I do! Make sure your profile is public. If you have a private profile, only people you accept can see your content. If you have things, you don`t want people to see on your profile, delete them and then make your profile public. Next, remember to post one or two posts a day. This will help the platform see that you are engaging and allow you to be seen more. Finally, you MUST respond to every single comment! It doesn`t matter if you respond with a heartfelt sentence or an emoji. Your posts get boosted when they are being engaged.

How can I go viral?

Going viral is really not up to anyone. You may see tips and tricks, and they may work, but most everyone is guessing. The best way to go viral is to stay consistent. The more videos and posts you have, the more likely you are to go viral. Once you have one video go viral, try to make another similar video and see what happens. Pro-tip, do not stop posting once you have a viral video. Keep your momentum going. Pushing a boulder up a hill is much easier once you have some momentum. However, it`s a thousand times harder to get going again once you stop.

I hate being on video; how can I get over this?

I know there are many of you who are afraid to post and be seen. I get it. I was there once too. Start by creating short videos where you talk about something for less than thirty seconds. Just because you record them doesn't mean you have to post them but get good at setting up your phone and pressing record. That really is the hardest part at first! The more you practice, the easier it will get. Utilizing Facebook and Instagram stories is a perfect starting point. You can even repurpose those into reels. This will help give you the extra confidence you need to keep going, show you that it's not as scary as you may think and easier than you may have imagined.

Coach's Notes: Jennie Jo's initial fear of being on video is a common obstacle for many aspiring network marketers. I want to reassure readers that feeling nervous at first is okay. Encourage them to start small with short videos and gradually build confidence. The art of storytelling, as exemplified by Jennie Jo, is a powerful tool for connecting with the audience. By honing their storytelling skills, they can captivate and engage potential customers as she did.

I can't begin to tell you what a life changer network marketing has been for me and my kids. If you have the desire and drive to go out and try these techniques I have shared with you, you can start to master the skills to be successful.

Your dreams are not only worth having, but they are achievable. I'm proof that our current situation, personality, experience, or background does not dictate our success. We can rewrite our story. I sure did, and you can too.

*"Your DRIVE
is born in your WHY!*

– Jenny

JENNY ERICSSON

- Hit the top rank on day one.

- Built a team in 10+ countries.

- Ten leaders in the team hit the top rank in one week.

- Started when I got fired and have built my business up to six figures since that day, from home around my kids.

Coach's Notes: Jenny's journey from being fired and facing burnout to becoming a top leader in the network marketing industry is truly inspiring. Her determination and willingness to embrace new strategies led her to the breakthrough she was seeking. As a leader, she understood the importance of setting clear goals and aligning her team with shared objectives. Her thirty-day system is a testament to the power of engagement, valuable content, and fostering

a sense of community within the group. Jenny achieved remarkable success by continuously duplicating this structure, impacting thousands across different countries. Bravo, Jenny! Your story is a beacon of hope and possibility for all aspiring network marketers.

It all began in June 2015, when my world was turned upside down. Freshly fired from my position as a sales manager, I couldn`t help but wonder how employment in Sweden, known for its security, had failed me. It was a harsh wake-up call, especially since I was already grappling with the aftermath of burnout syndrome, juggling the responsibilities of raising two young children and paying off a mortgage.

Sitting in my car outside the place that had once provided my financial stability, I felt an overwhelming emptiness. For the past decade, I had struggled to make ends meet as a young single mother, taking on any available job to keep a roof over our heads and food on the table. The previous two years had brought some stability with a full-time position at a well-established company. Finally, I could breathe easier, knowing my salary would cover our expenses. The job had its challenges, and I had even taken a leave of absence due to my health, but I managed to bounce back. Unfortunately, just as I regained my footing, the company underwent a workforce reorganization, rendering my services obsolete.

After gathering myself in the car, I returned home and turned to Facebook to share my sudden unemployment. Desperate for any leads, I asked if anyone knew of any opportunities. Little did I know that an answer would come just a few hours later. The following day, I found myself in a cozy coffee shop, meeting a woman who introduced me to an entirely unfamiliar industry—network marketing. As she spoke passionately about its advantages and endless possibilities, all I could think about was how I could regain the stability of my $3,000 monthly salary.

"How much more would you like to earn?" she asked, catching me off guard. "Can I really determine my income?" I responded, feeling slightly bewildered.

"Yes, if you`re willing to put in the work," she assured me, her eyes filled with determination. Coming from a high position in one of Sweden`s largest recruiting companies, she had given up her career to devote full-time to this industry—something about her conviction convinced me to give this opportunity a chance.

Eight years have passed since that fateful day, and I consider it my transformative period. The first network marketing company I joined was one of the veterans in the industry, but little did I know that their strategies were outdated and their bonus plan overly conservative. They imposed restrictions on social media marketing, which posed a challenge for someone like me. Online businesses were becoming popular, and the idea of marketing, posting, and social selling excited me. However, the company`s policies limited me to traditional methods. I held countless one-on-one meetings each week, traversed the state for business presentations in the evenings, and invested significant money. In six months, I achieved what was considered one of the top positions, and over the years, I climbed to the next rank. Yes, it took me several years to progress, but it earned me a reputation in the company as hardworking and dedicated. I even had the opportunity to deliver keynote speeches worldwide, which helped me grow as an individual. Despite my efforts, however, a major breakthrough eluded me.

After five years, I felt stagnant. My team wasn`t expanding, and the exhaustion of convincing people to join me. What had I done wrong? Everyone kept encouraging me, claiming I was close to reaching my goals. I decided to seek inspiration beyond the confines of the company and learn from successful individuals in the network marketing industry.

Everything in my life changed after investing $6,000 and completing a course on running a profitable and duplicatable online business. The knowledge I gained propelled me toward the six-figure salary I had been tirelessly pursuing for years. So, what was the game changer? It was a system built on clear action points that were easy to duplicate and follow. This well-designed strategy allowed the initial setup to be done once and replicated by other team members. It utilized the functions of various social media platforms, and it was truly eye-opening. I had been searching for this missing piece for all those years—an effective and modern system that could be easily duplicated.

Embracing this newfound strategy, I made the decision to leave my previous company and start fresh. Within a short span of time, my team grew rapidly, and a few months into my new venture, I achieved the prestigious Double Blue Diamond top rank, securing a spot in the top five of the entire company. I also experienced my first six-figure month of sales and helped nine leaders within my team reach the esteemed Diamond rank during that same period. When I transitioned to a company that aligned better with my values, I reached the top rank on my very first day!

If you`re reading these pages, I`m certain you`re eager to learn more about the system I utilize and how it has made all of this possible. Due to limited space, I will focus on my thirty-day system for expansion, goal attainment, and creating duplication and leverage in this chapter. I call it "Scale Your Business in thirty Days."

My system revolves around using Facebook groups, although you can choose any platform with similar functionalities that suit your preferences. Within the group, prospects gather in one centralized location, where they can find all the necessary information about your company`s products or services, testimonials, business presentations, compensation plans, and more. Every member of your team invites people to join, rapidly expanding the group's size. To enhance engagement and maintain interest, you can incorporate various challenges, live streams, or other engaging activities among the members. For instance, if you're in the health business, you could organize a free challenge for participants to engage in daily yoga sessions or take a walk for seven consecutive days, sharing their experiences with the rest of the group. At the end of the challenge, you can announce rewards, offering participants some free products to try out. This serves as both product marketing and generates curiosity about the business. Subsequently, you can follow up with leads, closing deals or achieving goals for that particular month. It's essential to design the challenge to make it accessible to everyone, encouraging maximum participation. Now, let's delve into the action steps for each week, providing a closer look at the process.

Coach's Notes: Jenny's thirty-day system revolves around the power of Facebook groups and their ability to create a centralized location for prospects to gather information about products, services, testimonials, business presentations, and compensation plans. The key lies in engaging leads through challenges, live streams, and other interactive activities that foster curiosity and excitement. Jenny nurtured a thriving community that drove growth and momentum by offering valuable content and maintaining a supportive presence. The importance of follow-ups and hosting impactful events cannot be underestimated. These steps ensure continuous engagement and foster an environment of inspiration and motivation. So, remember to adapt this powerful system within Facebook groups and watch your business scale to new heights.

Week 1 - Engage Leads in the Free Challenge

During the first week, your primary focus is on attracting leads and prospects who will be interested in joining the group. As the planner, you already have a clear idea of the challenge you'll be running in the second week. Now is the time to promote it on your social media platforms and extend invitations to individuals who would like to participate in the challenge.

Simultaneously, this is the opportune moment to set your monthly goal, which you aim to achieve by the end of the thirty-day scaling process. This goal could encompass various objectives, such as achieving rank advancements, increasing income levels, or expanding your team by recruiting new business owners. As a leader, I recommend providing marketing materials to your team to facilitate their promotional efforts online. By doing so, everyone can easily leverage these materials to attract more participants and generate interest in the challenge.

It is your responsibility as a leader to plan and communicate the monthly goals with your team and leaders. By aligning everyone with the same action goals for the month, you create a cohesive and focused environment where everyone is working towards shared objectives. This unity will foster a sense of camaraderie and drive within the team, ultimately propelling you closer to achieving your desired outcomes at the end of the month.

Week 2 - The Free 5-Day Challenge

In the second week, your main focus shifts toward the execution of the free challenge. This is an opportunity for you to foster engagement and interaction among the group members. Take advantage of live streams to provide valuable trainings or deliver speeches on specific topics that resonate with the participants. By offering free value, you'll create a sense of appreciation among the members and establish yourself as a knowledgeable and supportive leader.

Maintaining an active presence within the group during this week is crucial. Share your participation in the challenge and regularly comment on the progress and efforts of your team and your leads. By actively participating and providing guidance, you will reinforce the sense of community and encourage the members to stay involved.

Additionally, this week marks the beginning of promoting the upcoming event scheduled for the following week. Start building anticipation and generating interest around this event by creating buzz within the group. Share teasers, sneak peeks, or hints about what the event entails, igniting curiosity and excitement among the members. This strategic promotion will maximize attendance and participation in the event, ensuring its success.

By focusing on creating engagement, delivering valuable content, and building anticipation for the next event, you will keep the momentum strong and continue to drive growth and enthusiasm within the group.

Week 3 - Follow Up & Event

In the third week, you`ll engage in two key activities. The first is to follow up with the leads you generated during the free challenge. Connect with them through Messenger, WhatsApp, or any other platform you use, and guide them toward your products or services. It`s essential to nurture these relationships and address any questions or concerns they may have. As a bonus, consider organizing a giveaway within the group for all the participants. People love the opportunity to win something, enhancing their engagement and enthusiasm.

The second action step for this week is to host the monthly event, which can be conducted in person or online. As the team leader, you will collaborate with your leaders to plan and create this event. This involves determining the date, time, location (if applicable), agenda, and speakers. The event`s primary focus is to extend invitations to your team members and prospects. This event serves as a powerful platform to showcase the vibrant energy of the team, provide more detailed information about the company, products, or services, and share impactful testimonials. Furthermore, it is an opportunity to recognize the achievements of individuals who have attained rank advancements or put in significant effort.

The event acts as a catalyst for inspiration, motivation, and further education within the team and among prospects. By attending, individuals experience firsthand the positive atmosphere, gain valuable insights, and witness the rewards of hard work and dedication. It is a pivotal moment that strengthens the bond among team members and generates excitement and enthusiasm for the business opportunity.

This week, your focus should be executing follow-ups with leads and inviting them to the event. This ensures their continued engagement and gives them a comprehensive understanding of the company and its offerings. By combining the personal touch of follow-ups with the impactful experience of the event, you create a powerful foundation for growth and success within your team.

Week 4 - Momentum Week

The final week, Momentum Week, is when you and your team channel all the energy and movement that has been building throughout the month to achieve your monthly goals. If your company has a monthly offer or promotion, utilize it to drive momentum. If not, you can create incentives and rewards to keep the enthusiasm high. This week is not meant for relaxation; it`s a time to push forward and finish the month strong.

During Week 4, focus on follow-ups with leads, conducting team calls, hosting Q&A sessions, and supporting your team members in achieving rank advancements. The growth of your team directly contributes to your growth, so it`s crucial to foster their success. Start with yourself and then duplicate the strategies and actions to your team, leaders, and potential future leaders. This duplication is key to scaling your business effectively.

I have personally duplicated this structure with my leaders, and they have further replicated it in various countries and languages without my direct involvement at every step. By following this strategy month after month, we have amassed over 40,000 leads in our groups and witnessed the duplication of success in over ten countries. With over 500 new ranks achieved, including many top ranks, throughout the years, this strategy has led to success.

Embrace the energy and momentum that has been cultivated throughout the month and direct it towards the accomplishment of your goals. Stay focused, continue building your team, and drive towards success as you wrap up the month on a high note.

If you adopt this monthly structure, you will not only scale your business for a single thirty-day period, but you will do so continuously every month! This system provides clear action steps that everyone in your team can follow, ensuring consistent monthly results. It fosters duplication and leverage, which lie at the core of Network Marketing. The ultimate goal is to work yourself out of the process, allowing your business to grow independently.

Coach's Notes: One of the most remarkable aspects of Jenny's success is the power of duplication. She empowered her team to achieve incredible results even in her absence by implementing a system that is easy to follow and replicate. This key principle lies at the core of network marketing. Jenny's story serves as a testament to the fact that a well-designed strategy, combined with dedication and teamwork, can lead to exponential growth. So, embrace the power of duplication, set clear action goals, and witness your business soar to new heights every month.

CONGRATULATIONS TO YOU! Your efforts have laid the foundation for a thriving business that can generate ongoing success. By implementing this strategy, you have successfully scaled your business, and now the true essence of freedom begins to take hold.

"The likability factor is often the X-factor that sets successful people apart. It can be the tipping point in decision-making."

– Brian Tracy

KAT RITTER

- Had many accomplishments in the arts and publishing. Had shows in LA, New York, and across Europe.

- Has a wide fan club base as a Jazz musician.

- Has been able to use her accomplishments to connect with people and help them find their passion.

Leveraging Likability

In the business world, a powerful factor can greatly influence your path to success—likability. Beyond the quality of your products or the brilliance of your ideas, being genuinely likable can give you a significant edge in building relationships, attracting opportunities, and achieving long-term prosperity. Likability encompasses more than being pleasant or affable; it involves connecting with others, inspiring trust, and creating lasting impressions. This chapter will explore the vital role of likability in business and uncover practical strategies to enhance this essential trait, ultimately propelling you toward greater professional success.

Success heavily relies on building strong relationships and connecting with people on a deeper level. Being genuinely likable is a crucial aspect of achieving this. In this chapter, we will explore the key principles shared by an experienced network marketer on effortlessly becoming more likable and attracting others to your business.

The Likability Advantage

In the competitive landscape of network marketing, a powerful advantage exists that can set individuals apart and propel them toward success—the Likeability Advantage. It goes beyond traditional measures of competence and expertise, encompassing the innate ability to connect with others on a genuine and personal level. The Likeability Advantage is the secret ingredient that can unlock doors, forge strong relationships, and open up a world of opportunities. The intangible quality attracts people and inspires trust, loyalty, and collaboration.

Cultivating the Likeability Advantage can lead to a thriving and sustainable business. By actively practicing active listening, embracing a servant mindset, and demonstrating emotional intelligence, you can enhance your likeability and elevate your interactions to a higher level. When people feel heard, valued, and understood, they are more likely to view you as a reliable and approachable partner. Your ability to empathize and connect with others builds rapport and establishes a sense of camaraderie, making it easier to inspire and motivate your team members to achieve their goals.

The Likeability Advantage is not confined to interpersonal relationships within your network. It can also extend to potential customers and clients. People who find you likable are more inclined to choose your products or services over your competitors. Positive interactions leave a lasting impact, leading to word-of-mouth referrals and recommendations that can boost your business's reputation and reach. The power of likeability cannot be underestimated in a world where relationships and trust play significant roles in business success.

The Likeability Advantage is a transformative quality that can significantly impact your network marketing journey. By embodying the principles of active listening, servant leadership, emotional intelligence, and maintaining a positive attitude, you can cultivate an irresistible likeability that draws people toward you and your business. The relationships you build, the trust you inspire, and your collaborative spirit will contribute to unparalleled success in your network marketing endeavors. Embrace the Likeability Advantage and witness how it propels you toward extraordinary achievements and a thriving network that stands the test of time.

As you embark on your network marketing journey, understanding the six key concepts of likeability can significantly impact your success. The more you embrace these concepts, the more you will cultivate strong relationships, foster customer loyalty, and build a powerful personal brand that sets you apart in network marketing. Let's jump into the six key concepts!

Coach's Notes: The Likeability Advantage is a critical aspect of success in network marketing. You can set yourself apart and attract long-term prosperity by genuinely connecting with others, inspiring trust, and creating lasting impressions. Kat emphasizes the importance of building strong relationships, actively listening, and adopting a servant mindset to enhance likability. Remember, likability goes beyond charisma; it's about cultivating authentic connections and putting others' needs first. Embrace the power of likeability, and you'll naturally draw people to your business.

Building Trust and Rapport

Being likable creates trust and rapport, which is crucial in business interactions. When people perceive you as approachable, friendly, and genuine, they are more likely to feel comfortable working with you, sharing information, and engaging in mutually beneficial collaborations. Trust is the bedrock of successful relationships, and likability serves as a powerful catalyst in establishing that trust.

To become genuinely likable, adopt a servant mindset. Regardless of whether someone is a potential customer or a prospective team member, prioritize their needs over your own. Show genuine care and empathy towards others. Understand that when you put their best interests first, you earn their trust and create a positive and memorable experience. Being truly service-oriented will set you apart from those solely focused on your rank or success.

In network marketing, collaboration, and support are essential for success. Instead of obsessing over your own rank or achievements, focus on helping others achieve their goals. A rising tide lifts all boats, and when you invest in the growth and development of your team members, they become more committed and loyal. Celebrate their victories and offer guidance when needed. Becoming a mentor and cheerleader for others creates an environment of likeability and camaraderie.

Positive Attitude and Emotional Intelligence

Even in the face of adversity, maintaining a positive attitude can make a lasting impression on others. It demonstrates resilience, optimism, and the ability to navigate challenges gracefully. When you approach setbacks with a positive mindset, you inspire those around you to do the same. People are naturally drawn to individuals who exude confidence and optimism, especially in times of difficulty. Your positive attitude can become contagious, uplifting the spirits of your team members and customers alike. Moreover, a positive outlook can help you find creative solutions and turn obstacles into opportunities. Instead of dwelling on problems, you become a problem-solver, showing others that challenges can be conquered with the right mindset and approach.

Honing emotional intelligence allows you to understand and manage your emotions effectively and perceive and respond to the emotions of others. This skill fosters empathy, collaboration, and constructive relationships. Emotional intelligence enables you to connect with people on a deeper level, empathizing with their feelings and concerns. By understanding the emotions driving their decisions, you can communicate more effectively and tailor your approach accordingly. This heightened emotional awareness also helps you manage your reactions in high-stress situations, preventing impulsive actions or words that could damage relationships. When you display emotional intelligence, you create an atmosphere of trust and respect where people feel comfortable expressing themselves authentically. As a result, your network becomes a supportive community bonded by genuine connections and a shared sense of understanding and care.

Effective Communication and Active Listening

Being an effective communicator involves not only expressing your ideas clearly but also being an active listener. Listen to listen and not to speak. Listen attentively, ask insightful questions, and give others the space to express themselves fully. Seek to understand before being understood, and tailor your communication style to resonate with your audience. These practices will make others feel heard and valued, strengthening your connections.

One of the most common pitfalls in network marketing is over-talking and under-listening. It can be a major turnoff when you're too focused on leading the conversation in your desired direction without considering the other person's needs and desires. Remember, building rapport and trust begins with actively listening to others. By giving people a chance to express themselves and their aspirations, you can better understand how your products or business opportunity can truly help them.

By mastering the art of active listening, you can identify your prospects and team members` specific pain points and aspirations. This deeper understanding will allow you to tailor your approach and present solutions that genuinely resonate with their needs. When people feel that you genuinely care about their concerns and are willing to listen, they are more likely to trust you and be open to your recommendations. As a result, you`ll be able to build authentic connections and foster a supportive network where individuals feel valued and understood. The power of active listening is not to be underestimated, as it can be the key to unlocking the full potential of your network marketing journey.

Temperate Your Ego and Your Energy

Tempering one`s ego and sense of entitlement requires consciously cultivating humility and perspective. Firstly, it is essential to recognize that everyone has their own unique strengths and weaknesses and that no one is inherently superior to others. Practicing empathy and understanding toward others experiences and viewpoints can help foster a more balanced perspective. It is important to remember that accomplishments and success are not solely individual efforts but are often the result of teamwork and external support. Developing a mindset of gratitude and appreciation for the contributions of others can help reduce a sense of entitlement. Lastly, engaging in self-reflection and self-awareness exercises, such as meditation or journaling, can aid in recognizing and addressing ego-driven behaviors, allowing for personal growth and more harmonious interaction with the world around us.

In network marketing, success extends beyond product knowledge and marketing strategies. It also hinges on the energy you project into the world and the connections you create with others. This chapter delves into the significance of energy in network marketing, highlighting how being in a negative or boastful space can repel potential customers and team members. Conversely, embracing a servant mindset and selflessness can transform interactions and attract others effortlessly.

Understanding the Impact of Energy

Energy is an invisible force that influences our interactions with others. It's the vibe we exude, shaped by our thoughts, emotions, and actions. When we are in a negative or boastful place, that energy becomes palpable to those around us. Negativity can be contagious, and boastfulness can come across as self-centered and unappealing. Recognizing this impact is crucial to developing the self-awareness to project positive and inviting energy.

Some individuals make the mistake of putting themselves first and trying to make everything about them. While self-confidence is essential, an excessive focus on self-importance can alienate others. In network marketing it's vital to remember that success comes through genuine connection and service, not through an egocentric approach. People who sense a selfish vibe are less likely to trust and engage with such individuals.

Adopting a servant mindset can transform the way you interact with others. Rather than approaching relationships with an agenda centered on your own gain, focus on how you can be of service to others. Embrace a genuine desire to help and uplift those around you. When people feel your authentic care and support, they are more inclined to reciprocate and become active participants in your network.

Entitlement is toxic in any relationship, including business connections. No one owes you anything, and understanding this is critical to building authentic relationships. Instead of expecting favors or success to be handed to you, commit to earning trust and respect through your actions and dedication. Humility and gratitude will enhance your likability and foster strong bonds with your team and customers.

To project positive energy, start by taking care of yourself physically and mentally. Engage in activities that boost your mood and reduce stress. Cultivate an optimistic outlook, even in the face of challenges. Surround yourself with supportive and like-minded individuals who uplift you. By radiating positivity, you`ll attract individuals who appreciate your energy and share similar values.

The energy you put out into the world significantly impacts your success. Being in a negative or boastful place can repel potential customers and team members, hindering growth. However, embracing a servant mindset, selflessness, and positive energy creates an atmosphere of authenticity and connection. Remember that no one owes you anything; success is built on genuine relationships and mutual support. As you focus on serving others and fostering a positive environment, you`ll naturally attract like-minded individuals who share your vision, creating a network that thrives on trust, collaboration, and long-term success.

Coach's Notes: In this chapter, Kat delves into the impact of energy in network marketing. Your positive or negative energy can significantly influence your success. You create an atmosphere of authenticity and connection by tempering your ego, embracing humility, and projecting a servant mindset. Being genuinely likable is about building trust, demonstrating emotional intelligence, and offering value without being pushy. Show gratitude, be transparent, and uphold your values to build a strong personal brand that attracts clients, partners, and success.

Customer Loyalty and Repeat Business

Customers are more than just one-time transactions, they are the lifeblood of your business. When customers like you and enjoy the experience of doing business with you, they are more likely to become loyal patrons and advocates for your brand. Word-of-mouth referrals, positive reviews, and repeat business can be the result of the likability factor.

Pushy sales tactics can alienate potential customers and team members. Instead, embrace the art of the soft sell. Educate people about your products or business opportunity without putting pressure on them to buy or join immediately. Offer value by sharing insights, tips, and resources that can genuinely help them. People appreciate authentic connections and are more likely to engage with someone who is passionate about serving their needs.

Authenticity is also a magnet for likeability. Embrace your true self and be transparent in your interactions. People appreciate honesty and integrity. Share your journey, including both successes and challenges, to create relatability. Being vulnerable and genuine allows others to connect with you on a deeper level and builds trust in your character and intentions.

Coach's Notes: Likability plays a crucial role in establishing trust and rapport with customers, making them more likely to become loyal patrons and advocates for your brand. Embrace the art of the soft sell, educate without pressure, and be authentic in your interactions. Investing in your personal brand will boost your credibility and attract like-minded individuals who appreciate your genuine approach. Remember, likeability is the key to lasting success in network marketing.

Building a Strong Personal Brand

Investing in your personal brand can enhance your likability and reputation. Be consistent, uphold your values, and deliver on your promises. Build a reputation for reliability, integrity, and competence.

Engage in thought leadership activities, share valuable insights, and contribute to your professional community. Establishing a strong personal brand boosts your credibility and makes you more attractive to potential clients and business partners.

Being likable in business is not just a matter of charisma or being popular. It is about cultivating genuine relationships, building trust, and demonstrating empathy. Likability can help you stand out in a crowded marketplace and open doors to new opportunities. Remember, people do business with people they like, and by being likable you position yourself for long-term success in the world of business.

In the world of network marketing, becoming more likable is a powerful asset that will naturally attract customers and team members to you. You can create meaningful connections that transcend business transactions by honing your listening skills, adopting a servant mindset, helping others succeed, using soft selling techniques, and remaining authentic and transparent. Remember, when you genuinely care about others and prioritize their needs, your likeability will shine through, setting you on a path to lasting success in network marketing.

As you embrace the art of active listening, you`ll gain valuable insights into your prospects and team members` desires and aspirations. This deeper understanding will enable you to tailor your offerings to precisely match their needs, making your products or business opportunity all the more appealing. By genuinely empathizing with others, you can forge bonds based on trust, respect, and mutual support, forming a solid foundation for your network to thrive.

The servant mindset is not merely a business strategy; it`s a way of life that extends beyond the boundaries of your network marketing journey. When you put others first and focus on adding value to their lives, you`ll witness a positive ripple effect in every aspect of your interactions. The trust you build will translate into loyalty, with team members and customers remaining committed to your vision and your products. Your reputation as a selfless leader will attract like-minded individuals who share your values, contributing to the organic growth of your network.

Soft selling is an art that allows you to bridge the gap between your offerings and your customer's needs without the pressure of a hard sell. By providing valuable information and focusing on how your products can genuinely improve the lives of others, you'll earn a reputation as a trusted advisor rather than a pushy salesperson. This approach cultivates a sense of authenticity that people find refreshing, making them more receptive to your message and more likely to engage in meaningful conversations.

Remaining authentic and transparent is essential in network marketing, where honesty and integrity form the bedrock of lasting relationships. When you are genuine and true to yourself, people can sense your sincerity, making it easier for them to trust and connect with you. Transparency in your communication builds credibility, ensuring that your team members and customers are well-informed about the opportunities and challenges they might face. Your authenticity will act as a beacon, attracting individuals who appreciate your openness and align with your mission.

In conclusion, mastering the art of likeability in network marketing is not about adopting superficial techniques to win people over. It's about genuinely caring for others, actively listening, serving with humility, and authentically engaging with your audience. When you prioritize your team's and customer's needs, you create a supportive and collaborative environment that fosters growth and success for all. Embrace the power of likeability, and watch as your network marketing journey transforms into a fulfilling and rewarding adventure driven by meaningful connections and a shared sense of purpose. With likeability as your guide, you'll be well on your way to leaving a lasting legacy of positive impact and genuine success in the world of network marketing.

"Everything you want is on the other side of fear."

— Jack Canfield

LIZ STRULOWITZ

- Ranked up four times in my first six months.

- Leading a half a million dollar team.

- Regularly recognized in my Team`s Monthly Top 20 in Sales Leaderboard.

Face Your Fears and Get Over Yourself – How to Approach Prospects

Get over my fears? "Sure, okay, no problem," you say as you roll your eyes. We all know that fears can be debilitating, and we all have them. Whether you`re considering joining a Network Marketing business or are a seasoned professional in the NWM industry, I`m sure you experience some form of fear regularly, maybe even daily.

Coach's Notes: Liz starts by acknowledging the universal challenge of overcoming fears in network

marketing. As she addresses the fear of inviting people to join a team, she emphasizes the importance of coming from a place of service and genuinely believing in the opportunity for others. Her experience with a loyal customer demonstrates the value of persistence and a service-oriented approach. The key takeaway from Liz's insights is to "get over yourself" and remember that offering an opportunity multiple times doesn't equate to being pushy. Trusting the process and facing fears head-on can lead to significant growth in the network marketing business.

The biggest fear I see over and over again in this industry is in regard to building a team. So many of us are afraid to ask people to join our team. The most common reasons I hear are, "I don't want people to be angry with me," "I'm afraid of rejection," "I'm worried what people will think of me," "What if I say the wrong thing and the person says no," "I don't even know how to bring it up/start the conversation," I don't want to be pushy," and plenty of others. Do any of these sound like you?

Believe me, most of this is just your inner dialog messing with you and has no basis in reality. Let me ask you this...if a friend of yours started working at a company and said, "I just started working for this company, and I love the culture, my co-workers, the training, and the pay! If you're looking for a new place to work, you should totally check it out!", would you think she was being pushy? Would you get angry at her and think she has some nerve to suggest you apply for a job at her company? Do you think she'd be crushed if you said you're not interested? If you have any interest in joining her company, do you think she could say anything wrong? Probably not. You would ask more clarifying questions to learn more about the position.

Do you see where I'm going with this? It's really no different with Network Marketing. I'll let you in on the two biggest "secrets":

1) Come from a place of service-You offer the opportunity to people because you see it as a great opportunity for THEM, NOT because you're desperately trying to build your team for personal gain.

2) No just means "not now"; it doesn't mean no forever.

Coach's Notes: The chapter presents valuable advice on how to approach potential recruits, focusing on a service-oriented and authentic manner. It highlights the significance of understanding individual needs and aligning the opportunity with their interests. The analogy of recommending a job opportunity to a friend beautifully illustrates the non-pushy approach.

I have a customer who absolutely loves the products I sell. Since she's such a big fan, I asked her if maybe she would like to sell it too. She said thanks, but no thanks. I know it's hard to believe, but I survived the experience of being rejected. A few months later, after she placed a large order, I approached her again, saying that even if she were not interested in selling, she would save a lot of money by joining the company because she would always get her products at 25% off. She again declined the offer. Every few months, I would approach her and say, "I'm not trying to be pushy; I'm really trying to help you save money," and offer the opportunity to her again. She kept saying no, and I couldn't understand why for the life of me. I mean, who doesn't like to save money? I lived in fear, too. I didn't want to be pushy and scare her away. She was one of my best customers, and I appreciated her business and what had become a friendship. That's why I waited a few months and only approached her as a benefit to HER. Again, after a particularly large order, I reached out to her again, and she said she wasn`t interested. Instead of shying away, I said, "Can I just ask you why you`re not interested? You could be saving so much money." She said she didn`t want to pay the $10 website fee! I was floored! I did the math for her and showed her that even after paying that $10 fee, she would have saved about $90 on her last order. She was surprised, too, and appreciated that I showed her the numbers. Guess what? She STILL didn`t join! Too funny! But then, my company offered some amazing special on the starter kit, and she said, "I really think I need to join now!" She did!

Coach's Notes: I love how this chapter emphasizes the significance of confronting fears and expanding one's comfort zone to achieve success in network marketing. By encouraging readers to "expand their comfort zone" and embrace discomfort as part of learning, Liz motivates us to take intentional action daily.

I shared this story to illustrate how presenting an offer to someone multiple times doesn`t mean you`re being pushy, "no" just means "not now," and I didn`t scare her away or make her angry at me. It also demonstrates one way to approach someone about a business opportunity. I was coming from a place of service, so my approach was genuine and authentic, not forced.

There are other ways to approach the offer in a very non-threatening or scary way that I will discuss a little later. I`ll be honest when I first started in Network Marketing, I was very excited about selling the products but lived in fear about offering the business opportunity. When I did, I made the mistake of talking WAY too much about all the benefits. It`s really important to ask questions and listen and then respond accordingly. Not everyone will want to join your company for the reasons you did. Find out what their needs are and see how your company can be a solution to their problems (extra income, feeling valuable, filling a void, being able to connect with a whole network of teammates, making new friends, living life with a purpose, etc.). Don`t let fear get in the way of you helping people get what they want or need. What if nobody ever approached YOU with the opportunity? I never would have thought about joining if I hadn`t been asked. This is what I mean by "get over yourself." It`s really not about you at all. It`s about you being the medium in which to help another person.

Here`s some good advice...don`t be the person you`re afraid of becoming. In other words, if you don`t want to be pushy, then don`t be pushy. Don`t be rude or nasty if you don`t want people to get angry with you. That being said, don`t think of yourself as being pushy or rude by offering the opportunity for people to look at the business. If you`re truly coming from a place of service, you may be offering something that will completely change their lives for the better. Never prejudge! Don`t assume that a person wouldn`t be interested in what you have to offer because of their current life circumstances. You have absolutely no idea what someone is thinking or needing unless you talk to them about it.

If you`re new to Network Marketing and you`re wondering how to build a team, it helps to make a few lists of people you`d like to approach. Think of stay at home moms who are looking for something to do that they can call their own. Think of retired adults who still want to be productive and earn some extra income. Think of wildly popular people or trendsetters who people gravitate towards and want to do everything they`re doing. Think of people who are natural-born sellers that just have the knack. Think of friends you would love to go through your business journey with. Think of people who are lonely and would love to have a built-in network of teammates (and customers) to be able to connect with. With each of these groups of prospects, there`s really a very simple approach to discussing joining your Network Marketing team.

When you go through your lists, if there are certain people you REALLY want to work with, put a star next to their name and write down WHY you really want them on your team. Call them up (a voice clip is not ideal, but the next best option. Never send a text message about the business opportunity) and be honest. Say something like, "Hey, Jill. This may or may not be right for you, but I just started working for this company and thought of you. You would be so good at this because ____ (fill in the blank). Because these products are so YOU (explain why) because you`re so good with people, you`d be a total natural at this because it would be so much fun to work together because I know you have little kids. You`ve been looking to do something just for you and not about the family. By saying, "This may or may not be right for you," you take the pressure off them, allowing them to relax and listen to what you say. You can also add, "If not for you, maybe you know someone this would be perfect for.".

When you`re really nervous about approaching someone about your business, especially people you don`t know well, you can start or finish by saying, "I`d rather you say "no" than you be upset with me for never offering you this opportunity." When using this approach, not only have I not put people off, but they actually thanked me for reaching out even though they aren`t interested (at this time). Another way to approach prospects can come up easily and naturally. People often bring up their jobs in natural conversation, and in many cases, they`re complaining about their jobs. That`s a perfect opportunity to ask, "Have you ever thought about doing what I do?" I can`t think of a more natural, non-threatening way to bring up the topic. Either the person already knows what you do, or they`re going to ask. Again, this isn`t an opportunity to launch into a huge monologue about your business. Usually, less is more. Let people ask you more about what you do and find out what the benefits are of joining your company. I could write another chapter about the art of prospecting, but this one focuses on facing your fears.

Even when you face your fears and offer the business opportunity, statistically, you're still going to get rejected more often than not. That's okay. Your business isn't for everyone, just like you may not want to be a Pharmacist or a Swim Instructor. You really have no reason to take it personally and shouldn't. You have to think of your business the same way. Your offering of a great opportunity won't resonate with everyone, and it doesn't have to. Keep at it, and you'll find your people.

With all the advice I've given here, I bet you're still nervous, and that's okay. Do you know how to overcome it? DO IT ANYWAY!! I used to say, "Get out of your comfort zone," but now I say, "Expand your comfort zone." The only way to do that is by getting uncomfortable and doing it anyway. Trust me, the more you approach people, the more you will be cultivating your skills, and eventually, you will feel more confident in what you're doing. It's like that with everything that's new and uncomfortable. When you started working at your first job, I'm sure you were nervous and probably weren't great at it. But over time, you learn how to do your job better through trial and error and gaining more skills. It's no different with Network Marketing Companies. There's always a learning curve at a new job, but eventually, you get the hang of it, plus you have the benefit of a whole team to help you learn and succeed.

The worst thing would be to look back at your life and realize that you never reached your full potential because your fears held you back. But what would happen if you faced your fears? Imagine the life you could have if you didn't let your fears paralyze you. The time is now to start living the life you were meant to live. It's all mindset. Decide today that you're not going to live in fear any longer because you want to live your best life. Your potential is endless.

"Don't count the days;
make the days count!"

— Muhammad Ali

MARGARET ANNE NEWSOME

- Joined network marketing in 1997.

- Built a global organization.

- Top 1% of two network marketing companies.

- Serial Entrepreneur.

- Real Estate Broker/Investor.

Time Management-Set Yourself Up for Success

Time management is a misunderstood concept. You don`t "manage time." You make choices and prioritize your focus. Every day, whether you realize it or not, you prioritize one thing over another. Time is a non-renewable resource. We all have the same 24 hours in a day. How you choose to use those 24 hours makes a difference.

When you begin to look at time management, it`s important to ask yourself, what are you spending your time on? Are you spending your time doing what you want to do? Or are you spending your time doing what others want you to do? Think about that. Is what you are doing bringing you closer to your goal? Or closer to someone else's goal? It's time to take a good hard look at how you spend your time.

Start with you. Are you making yourself and your goals a priority? Know that it's okay to do so. In fact, it's necessary to prioritize your physical, mental, and emotional health. Set boundaries. Learn to say no. Ensure you eat, sleep, rest, schedule downtime, and have fun. Your health is an investment, not an expense. Self-care is essential. Prioritizing yourself will help you have more brain power and energy to focus on doing what you need each day. A great analogy is like when the oxygen mask falls on an airplane; you put the mask on yourself first so that then you can help others. You have to take care of yourself. If you don't, eventually, it will catch up with you. Take my word for it, I learned that the hard way.

When I started network marketing in 1997, my dear friend and mentor Debra said, "Meet me at Applebee's at 11 am and bring your calendar. We are going to set you up for success."

Okay! Set me up for success, I thought; how exciting! I wasn't going to just "get started." I was going to get set up to be successful. And I wasn't going to have to figure it out alone; she was going to help me and tell me how to do it. Fantastic!

This was a relief because failing was not an option. I needed to make money, but it was important that I have time flexibility. I wanted to stay home with my children. At the time, I had two boys, almost 2 and 4 years old, and I was pregnant with my daughter. I was working full-time. I had an opportunity to do something different, and I was taking it. I didn't want to miss out on my kids growing up. I showed up to Applebee's, calendar in hand, ready to listen and learn.

When I arrived, Debra said, "This is a business meeting; afterward, we can visit." This set the tone and expectations for what was about to happen. She said, "In order for me to best help you, I need to know where you are going. What do you want from this opportunity? Why are you here? What are your goals? Do you want a big business, a little business, or a hobby? There are no right or wrong answers." These questions were important because they helped me set goals and create the foundation and direction for what I was to do next.

Next, she asked, "How many hours do you want to work a week? 1-5? 5-10? Ten or more?" She proceeded to explain that a hobby would be 1-5 hours a week. A little business would be 5-10 hours a week, and a big business would be more than 10 hours a week. She took my appointment book (broken out into 15-minute increments) and set it in front of me. She said, "X off the time you sleep. Then fill in all the things you have to do each day. Schedule in your non-negotiables. Include your personal time and family time. What are you not willing to give up? Now, what hours do you want to work? You need to set business hours and make appointments with yourself to show up and do the work."

She explained that I didn't have to block off huge amounts of time at once. That it was possible to do 15 minutes here and there. Or an hour while the kids were napping. She also explained that time blocks could change according to our schedules and different phases of our lives. I wasn't locked into 9 to 5. I could make it work around my life and utilize my available time. She helped me do a time audit and realize that I could do many things differently to "create" plenty of time to build a business.

The skills I learned from Debra have not only helped me manage time for my network marketing business but have helped me manage life in general.

Coach's Notes: Margaret Anne's approach to time management goes beyond the conventional understanding. She wisely points out that time is a non-renewable resource, making our choices and priorities all the more critical. She highlights the importance of investing in ourselves by focusing on personal goals and self-care. Her emphasis on setting yourself up for success rather than merely getting started reflects her determination to achieve greatness in her network marketing journey. Margaret Anne's lessons resonate with the power of intention and mindful decision-making.

G-P-S: Goals, Plan, Schedule

- Goals-Know where you are going. Decide. Commit. Be disciplined. Be accountable. Celebrate accomplishments. Write down your goal. Make a vision board. Break big goals into smaller goals. Tell your family what your goals are and explain what`s in it for them. Be mindful not to get stuck just creating goals, go take action! You must actually go do the work.

- Plan-Reverse engineer how to reach your goal.

  What do you need to do in 90 days to reach your goal? What do you need to do each month? Each week? Each day? Break it down into action steps. What income-producing activities do you need to do daily to achieve your goal? Plan and be intentional. Plan your work and work your plan. I`ve heard Debra say that a gazillion times.

  Do a time inventory and audit. Become aware of what you spend your time on. Make a time map. Write down everything you do.

  Block pockets of time in your day. 15-minute chunks of time work great.

You can make phone calls or send messages within five, ten or fifteen minutes here and there.

Set a time each week to plan for the upcoming week. Sunday nights from 8 pm-10 pm works best for me.

Block time to batch tasks such as social media posts. Instead of trying to write a post every day, block off one hour and write several posts. Then you can schedule them to post each day.

Decide how many hours you want to work. Set your "work hours."

When you start to plan, do a brain dump and write down everything you are currently doing each day. Then lighten the load. Figure out what you can take off your plate.

This is what I call the WHAT-WHEN-WHO System:
—For each task you have, ask yourself, WHAT needs to be done?

Ask yourself, does this really need to be done? If so, move on to the next question. If not, delete it.

—If it needs to be done, WHEN does it need to be done? Does it need to be done today, tomorrow, this week? Or can it be done another time? If it can be done later, defer it. If it needs to be done in the next week, schedule it.

—Now ask, WHO needs to do it? Is it something you need to do yourself? Or can someone else accomplish the task? If someone else can do it, delegate it. Outsource it. Assign the task to someone else. Use Instacart, lawn care and cleaning services, automatic bill pay, and Fiverr. Use the time you would have normally spent on that task to do an income-producing activity. If you have to do it, schedule it.

• Schedule everything. This allows you to function with intention and purpose. If it`s not on the schedule, your brain will waste energy wondering when and how to accomplish the task.

Scheduling things provides clear direction and frees up brain power. When scheduling, be careful not to overcommit. Be sure to allow enough time in between tasks. Estimate each task's time and then add a little extra time. If you finish a task early, use that time to breathe and refocus. Taking short breaks helps get you back on task, and you will be more productive.

Keep in mind that "some day" and "one day" are not days of the week. "Sometimes" is not a time of the day. When scheduling, you must actually pick a date and time to do a task.

- Round-tuit story-One day, in my grandmother's kitchen, she tossed a wooden coin across the table. I caught it and said, "what's this?" She said, "That's your round tuit. People are always saying-I'll do it when I get around to it. Well, there's your round tuit." She just smiled. I realized I had to stop procrastinating. After all, now I had a round tuit—no more excuses. I decided I would take my round-tuit and go do it. Thanks, Nanny.

- Execute.

  - Commit to taking action every day. Be disciplined. Be accountable. Make choices, not excuses. Choose wisely.

  - Have a dedicated place to work. This helps you focus and be more productive.

  - Eliminate distractions—silence notifications. Use Do Not Disturb mode. If this freaks you out, you can still allow calls from "favorites" for kids, etc, to still get through in case of an emergency.

  - Use technology & tools.
    Timers are your friends. Use them! Stay on track!

  - Find a calendar or planner that works for you. I like paper. Some people prefer digital. I like to see and hold my planner and mark things off as I complete tasks. It gives me a sense of accomplishment. If digital is your thing, go for it! The main thing is to have a system that works for you. One that you will actually use.

- Use text replacement shortcuts on your phone and other devices. This is a huge time saver. Set up text replacements for things that you repeat often. It`s much quicker to type a few letters and a whole phrase or paragraph pop up instead of having to type everything out each time.

- Use voice clips. You can save them and use them over and over again to send information to people. Then you don`t have to keep saying the same thing over and over, but the recipient gets a personal touch hearing your voice. It`s like speaking directly to them.

- Use the shortcuts app on your phone. This app can schedule messages and posts.

- Repurpose content across different social media platforms so you don`t have to create new content for each platform. You can set up posts to go out to many platforms at one time.

- Automate repetitive tasks such as onboarding, training, sharing information, and tracking prospects and customers. Utilize a CRM (customer relationship manager) to help you.

- Use digital tools: Some of my favorites are the Boards app, Zoom, Vimeo, YouTube unlisted videos, Canva, and ChatGTP.

- Following a schedule will help reduce procrastination. You don`t have to think about what to do when or how to fit it all in. You already know what to do. Follow the schedule. Just do ONE thing. Then do the next one thing.

- Scheduling tasks and breaking work into smaller tasks helps reduce overwhelm and procrastination. Doing smaller tasks will help keep you consistent and productive.

- Establish daily routines. Routines are key. A routine is a sequence of actions followed regularly. Routines help reduce decision fatigue and establish habits. Routines become muscle memory. Have a routine for waking up, getting dressed, and leaving the house. Have an evening routine, down to brushing your teeth. Routines contribute to maximizing your time and being productive.

- Evaluate & adjust

  At the end of each week, sit down and review your productivity for the week. Notice what worked well and what needs to be adjusted. Tweak accordingly. Plan for the next week. The best time management system is the one that works for you and the one you will actually use. Try, tweak, repeat. Keep doing this until you find what works for you.

Your current actions are determining your future.

Time management isn`t one more thing you have to do. It`s how you do it. It`s how you get things done. Be proactive, not reactive. Be intentional. You`ve got this!

Coach's Notes: The G-P-S system explanation by Margaret Anne is a compass for effective time management. Her emphasis on setting clear and measurable goals resonates with the most successful individuals. Breaking these goals down into actionable plans enables better focus and consistency. Margaret Anne's practical time allocation strategies, such as time blocking and utilizing small time pockets, demonstrate adaptability in managing daily tasks. The use of technology and tools empowers efficiency and delegation, allowing individuals to maximize productivity. By promoting routines and rituals, she acknowledges the role of habits in optimizing time usage. Pay close attention!

Notes from Debra

1. Be present-whatever you are doing, do that. Be present and enjoy.

2. Put support systems in place. Make a plan for household chores, meals, and children. Just go ahead and know that you cannot do it all. I`ve tried. You will be way ahead to accept the reality that you need help, which is perfectly okay.

3. Celebrate wins-Celebrate the milestones, even the small steps. Include your family.

4. Take care of what bothers you. If something is a distraction, get rid of it. If you need to take a day and clean your house or car, do it! Clear the clutter and clear your mind.

5. Mail/email- touch it once. Use the TAR system-Trash it, take action, handle whatever it is, or file it for reference later. Check email at certain times of the day, not all day.

6. It`s important to be open to change. Things will remain the same until the pain of remaining the same is greater than the pain of change.

7. Learn to say no and understand it`s okay to do so. This can be difficult if you are a people pleaser. Learn to say, "Thank you for asking, but I have a previous commitment." Remember you have a commitment to yourself, and that`s okay.

8. Teach people how to treat you. You must first respect your time before others will.

9. Stop making yourself available to handle other people`s problems.

10. Use the 2-minute rule. If you can complete the task in 2 minutes, go ahead and do it. If it takes longer than 2 minutes, schedule it.

11. Stop doing it if it`s not moving you toward your goal or helping your family.

12. Stay focused-If your mind is wandering, stop for 2 minutes, then get back on track.

13. Have something to do in case you have to wait somewhere like the carpool line, doctor`s office, or train. Use your time wisely.

14. Keep a notepad and a pen beside your bed. The best ideas often come in the middle of the night.

15. Have the faith of a mustard seed.

Coach's Notes: Margaret Anne's closing notes summarize the chapter's essence, emphasizing the transformative nature of effective time management. Her coaching inspires readers to view time management as a way of life rather than just a set of techniques. One can harness the power of time by choosing to be proactive, intentional, and open to change. Her message to have the faith of a mustard seed speaks to the strength and unwavering belief required to succeed in any endeavor. Margaret Anne's teachings empower individuals to embrace time as a tool for shaping a successful future.

"Your influence is determined by how abundantly you place the other people's interests first."

— Bob Burg

MEGHAN BRAZIER

- Joined network marketing in August 2017.

- Top seller and recruiter in her company in her first year.

- In the top 1% of all network marketers with a seven-figure sales business.

- Lead speaker at her company convention.

- She has spoken on stage along with Ray Hidgon and other industry leaders at the yearly Attraction Marketing event in Vegas.

15 Steps to Becoming More Influential on Video so More People Want to do Business With You!

Building influence isn`t about flexing your authority but rather inspiring others to unlock their capabilities and create significant transformation.

Influence goes beyond the realm of being a popular 'influencer` with the perfect home, an impeccable hat collection, and the ideal image filters... It`s about cultivating a sense of trust with your audience. Here`s the uplifting truth: the ability to build influence is a skill that absolutely ANYONE can learn. It`s not a trait that you need to be born with.

If you haven`t already noticed, the larger the circle of people who know, like, and trust you, the greater the number of individuals who will want to engage in business with you.

So, what defines an influential figure from your perspective?

Reflect on individuals who have influenced you, and identify what exactly about them leaves such a profound impact.

Intriguingly, many of the influential people you may be considering started from scratch. They didn`t have the privilege of being born into extraordinary circumstances or enjoying a fairytale childhood.

For example, Oprah.

She was born into poverty and faced a lot of challenges throughout her childhood. But she persevered and went on to become an influential talk show host, philanthropist, and media mogul. She is now one of the most influential women in the world.

Or how about J.K Rowling? She became a household name as the author of the Harry Potter series. Before that she was a struggling single mother living on welfare. Publishers rejected her countless times, but she remained persistent in pursuing her dream of becoming a famous writer. She is now one of the most influential authors of our time. She demonstrates that one`s background or circumstances do not limit success.

I had a happy and loving childhood, but I was painfully shy. I barely spoke and would hide behind my parents. As I went through school, I was always the 'quiet' one. I feared speaking in public more than death.

If you had told me then that I`d be speaking on a stage in Vegas to a room full of network marketers...or at my company convention in front of thousands of consultants, I would have died at the thought!

If you would have told me I would be leading a network marketing team and people applying to join me because of the influence I have created or that I would build a coaching business from the ground up that people would pay a lot of money to get access to, I definitely would have thought you were crazy.

So what changed?

I developed skills along the way.

I pushed myself out of my comfort zone and got better and better.

You can learn these skills too.

When you do, it`s going to transform your business over time.

I will share with you fifteen skills you can learn starting today that anyone can learn to build their influence and attract people to them.

If you don`t know by now, video is the fastest way to grow influence. Whether it`s live video, short-form video, or simply in your stories, video is where you are going to build trust the fastest.

So let`s get into what these skills are!

1. Smile More

Smiling makes a huge difference as it can have numerous benefits. It portrays you as approachable, confident, and trustworthy. People are more likely to feel comfortable working with or doing business with someone who exudes warmth and positivity. Smiling can leave a lasting impression and help build a strong professional network.

I used to never smile much. I remember being younger and random people just telling me to smile as they walked by. Kinda weird now I think about it, but it`s always stuck with me. I make a way more conscious effort to smile, especially when meeting new people. People think you`re standoffish and won`t want to talk to you if you don`t smile! Smiling is a universal sign of friendliness and approachability. Smiling at others (even on camera) signals that you are open to communication and connection. It can break down barriers and encourage people to engage with you. Smiling creates a welcoming aura that helps foster and strengthen new relationships.

So start smiling more!

2. Saying (and Remembering) People's Names

Using someone`s name creates a sense of familiarity and closeness. It helps to establish a personal connection and encourages meaningful conversations. Remembering names allows you to build stronger relationships, as it shows that you care enough to remember and recall important details about others.

How did it feel when you commented on a live video you were watching, and that person called out your name to respond to you?

It immediately makes you like them more and deepens the connection.

I remember meeting a girl in my street who lived down the road. Usually, I`m not one to remember names, but I had learned how important this was, so I made a conscious effort to remember it. I saw her at the park a couple of weeks later and greeted her by saying her name. She was so shocked and genuinely impressed that I remembered her name.

She ended up being an amazing client of mine!

Remember, when you remember someone`s name, it shows them that you value their presence. It helps to establish a good first impression and fosters a sense of trust and credibility, making it easier to connect and collaborate with others.

3. Eye Contact

Eye contact is often associated with trustworthiness and credibility. It conveys honesty and sincerity and helps to establish trust with your audience. If you keep looking away, it`s easy to lose that connection. Have you ever had a conversation with someone when they kept looking away? It doesn`t make you feel very important. Or have you watched someone doing a live, and they aren`t looking into the camera enough? You lose connection quickly.

4. Body Language

Body language is speaking without words. Research shows that the majority of communication is non-verbal. When your body language aligns with your spoken words, it adds authenticity and reinforces your message. In building influence, consistency between verbal and non-verbal cues is crucial!

When I`m talking on camera, I make sure to use my hands to emphasize what I`m saying. If I just sat there and kept talking without using any body language, it would be boring and unengaging. So think about using your hands.

I saw a guy talking on the phone the other day, and he was pacing up and down the street, talking and using big gestures with his hands.

Even though the person on the other end of the phone couldn`t see him, those gestures helped him get his message across more intently. He was very involved in whatever story he was telling on that phone! Remember, we use body language to convey a message.

Coach's Notes: Meghan's transformation from a shy child to an influential figure speaks volumes about personal growth. Her journey shows that influence isn't about natural charisma but cultivating trust, connection, and respect. Remember, as Meghan proves, anyone can grow their influence, regardless of background. Influence is earned, not given. Every interaction counts. Learn from Meghan's lessons and watch your influence expand.

5. How you use Your Voice

Your tonality, your volume, the speed, all of these things matter. Your tempo, inflection, the variance, like whispering, leaning in, getting a bit quieter, pausing when you`ve got an important thing to say. Being clear, being louder when you need to be, being softer when you need to be.

Pausing when you need to be pausing. All these things make a difference in how you engage with people and your influence.

I had a coaching client who was struggling on camera. She had extremely low views on her videos, and I knew why. They were not engaging to watch. Her voice was monotone. She just sat there without a smile and barely used any body language. She wasn't excited at all to be there! Why would anyone want to watch it? It was boring!

So we started working on these skills, and her views picked up over time. She was more fun to watch and guess what...she started even making more sales from her videos.

6. Storytelling: Make Sure you Share your Personal Stories, and don't Forget to be Vulnerable Once in Awhile!

You need to inject your stories into your content. Stories build trust. Stories sell.

When I first started sharing my IVF journey, it was incredible how many people I was able to connect with. My story resonated with them and made them feel heard. It built trust with my audience.

When you have trust with your audience, they are way more likely to do business with you.

It's difficult to be vulnerable at first, but when you realize how much it helps others, it's worth it.

Over the years, I've used my experiences in day-to-day life as inspiration for my content. With practice, my storytelling has become a lot better. Adding in personal stories, using eye contact and body language, and ensuring my voice is engaging are all things that keep growing my influence!

You should start thinking about what stories you can use from your life that relate to the topic you want to teach or share with your audience! You don't always have to be vulnerable, though.

One of my favorite stories I share to teach my network about the importance of customer service is that of my nail salon. There are literally hundreds of nail salons in my area, but I still drive a good twenty minutes to get to mine.

Why do I go so far out of my way to go there?

The customer service is incredible, and they do a great job with my nails. They remember my name. They make me feel welcome, are professional, and offer free drinks. It`s just a vibe that I want to be in.

So I tell my audience...

"That`s how you want your customers to feel. They could shop with anyone. Why should they shop with you?"

When you throw in a story to really reiterate the message and the skill you`re trying to teach, that makes people lean in and listen and subsequently remember that skill. I always find when I`m listening to a training that if the speaker is telling a story, I lean in and listen more. This is always the part of the training that I remember. I bet you do this too.

I teach this a lot to my students, and when they start to use stories to share their experiences about their products or business, that`s when people tune in to listen.

7. Humor!

Can you make people laugh? Now you might not be a natural comedian, and that is okay, but being silly, goofing around, and adding some sort of humor helps a lot.

Funny makes you money. I`m telling you. If you can make people laugh, they`re going to want to come back for more. They`re going to enjoy listening to you. So think about how you can add some humor to your content! Do you always have to be funny? No! But if you can tell a funny story/experience you had or share something funny your kids did, people will like that!

When one of my leaders and I did a live, we got the giggles. We had been laughing about something before we went live, and it came back to haunt us. But instead of stopping, we embraced it. We turned it into a blooper, and people loved it. It showed people the real us and what we were like to work with (we like to have fun, obviously!). That`s the type of people we attract to our team. People who like to laugh and have fun.

8. Engaging with your Audience

Building influence is a two-way street. Encourage your audience to comment, share, and interact with your videos. Respond to comments promptly, address questions, and foster a sense of community. Engaging with your audience builds relationships and shows potential clients that you care about their input and value their engagement.

If you can ask your audience more effective questions, for example, "What is it that you are struggling with out of these skills so far?" You will get more thoughtful responses and build more connections with your audience. Understanding what they need will also help you in future content to solve their actual problems.

Coach's Notes: Meghan highlights the importance of using your voice effectively to establish a more profound connection with your audience. She emphasizes the importance of tonality, speed, and timing in communication. Additionally, she insists on sharing personal stories to build trust and engagement and encourages the use of humor to attract and retain people's attention. Finally, she stresses the value of audience engagement as a vital part of building influence. Meghan's experiences prove that these skills can be learned and improved.

9. Simplicity-The Art of Clear Communication

You need to share content that is easy to listen to and/or read. If you`re going to get way too complicated and you don`t have a clear plan, it will be hard for you to communicate that simply.

I had a mentor once who confused me so much. I felt like she never answered my questions and just spoke around and around in circles. I couldn`t continue working with her because she complicated everything.

When I am on social media teaching my audience something or leading a team meeting, I think about how I can most succinctly explain the information I want to share. Sometimes I`ll do a story sequence explaining the benefits of the products I`m using or my business opportunity. Quite often, I think, that was way too much information and too complicated. How can I do this again much more simply?

One of the best compliments I receive is when people tell me: "Thank you for explaining it that way. You made it make so much sense!"

So make it make sense! Practice if you need to and get everything in order in your mind or in your notes so you can clearly communicate to others.

10. Authenticity

So often, we`re trying to be like everyone else. I think we are all guilty of this every now and then. If you`re always trying to keep up with someone else you follow, you`ll never attract your people!

We all get imposter syndrome. When I notice that I`m comparing myself to someone else, I have to remind myself, "Meghan, your people aren`t here for them; they`re here for you."

I was talking to my coaches not too long ago, and I said to them... "I just feel like a million people are sharing the same message; what makes me special? Why would people want to listen to me?"

They had to remind me..."Meghan, but the way you say it, the way you teach it, the way you do it resonates with so many people."

Then I remembered what a student said to me once... "I have learned from so many other coaches, but when I came to you, the way you taught it was so much more clear, and I could understand it."

I also had someone join my team who said she had no interest in joining any of the other big influencers in our company because she resonated with me the most.

It's so easy to compare yourself and think everyone else is better, but there are people there that want to learn from YOU.

So make sure you continue to be yourself. No one can share your message like you.

What do you bring to the table? Be you. Show up as you.. Don't worry about what other people are doing. Don't try and be like another person on the internet.

Yes, you can learn from other people and model some of the things they're doing, but in terms of your character, be okay with the fact that not everyone's going to like you. But guess what...you have to repel to attract. Your tribe is out there.

11. Passion

You have to show your enthusiasm. I often talk about this with my team when we are training on recruiting. You need to show up and be so passionate about why you decided to do it, why you love it, how it`s helping people, how it`s helping you, and how it`s helping your team...has it changed your life for the better??? Even if it`s just a small change so far, shout it from the rooftops!

Being so passionate is contagious. If you are not passionate about it, you probably aren`t showing up on social media because you don`t have a belief in what you are doing. If you`re struggling with the belief, you need to check yourself and remind yourself why you are doing it.

Do you believe you can achieve your goals? Do you believe your team can achieve their goals?

I knew my passion had dropped in my first Network Marketing company when I stopped talking about the usiness opportunity. So, as a result, I stopped recruiting. I didn`t have the belief that my team could win where I was.

When I aligned myself with a company that was a better fit for me, my passion was ignited. I had such high belief, and my team grew so quickly because they could feel my excitement.

The passion explodes when you believe in what you are doing in your company, your products, your team, and your message. When you align with that, the passion is just unstoppable. And when you have that passion, people are just drawn to it.

12. Visualization

Your thoughts are so incredibly powerful. You need to spend some time visualizing and thinking about yourself in the future. Where do you see yourself? Visualize yourself on holidays, in your dream home, at the top of your company, walking across the stage, etc. These things give you more power and, without realizing it, help you become more influential because you`re so confident in your growth.

You know where you are, and you know where you are going. Your confidence grows, and it boosts your energy. One of my students told me the other day that she shifted her energy in her stories to be more bubbly and enthusiastic, and her engagement went up. She had more people viewing and engaging, and more conversations started! She said she got herself more aligned and more passionate, and it was crazy how the engagement changed in just a little shift in her energy.

13. Repetition

How many times have you thought..."Oh, I can't say this again. I've said it way too many times. No one else wants to hear it."

I feel that all the time. I'm like, "How many times do I need to talk about this?

"Have I talked about these products too much? Am I talking too much about my business? Am I annoying people?"

If you are thinking this, chances are you aren't sharing enough!

Now there's a difference between sharing too much if all you do is push your products and opportunity on people. But if you're doing a good job of showing up every day (especially in your stories), sharing your day, sharing bits and pieces of your life, and sharing recommendations for different things, then there is absolutely no problem peppering in your products and business daily! Just remember to use your storytelling to do so.

I always tell my team to share from three areas daily:

1. Entertain your audience
2. Add value to your audience
3. Market to your audience

When you can pull from these three areas each day, your audience is never going to get bored and will come back for me.

Remember, they are probably only checking in with you sporadically. So just assume that no one has seen your message today, and you need to make sure they see it today, or they might miss it.

If they have seen it already, they need to hear it twelve times before it clicks in their head. So teach them about your products and business again and again and again.

Share the deal, what`s going on, the benefits, and the problems and solutions. Share, share, share, share in your stories, share it on your feed, share it on different platforms, and share it in an email.

Just make sure to add value and entertainment too!

People like to consume content in different ways, so repurposing your content is key. This chapter I`m writing was actually inspired by a live video I did on my FB group and FB Page. I also turned it into an email series, a reel, and a carousel post. The opportunities are endless!

14. Calls to Action

Are you putting calls to action at the end of your content? Calls to action can be so different. It can be as simple as, "Give me a thumbs up if you agree" during a live video. Or "send me a DM with the word 'training' if you want to access," or "send me a DM with the word 'skincare' if you need help in your skincare routine."

It could also be sending them to somewhere else: "Hey, go and check out my Facebook group for the extended version, or download this free guide" (and get them on your email list).

Or just a simple call to action like, "If this resonated with you, give me a yes."

People need to know what to do next. TELL THEM!

Don`t just leave them hanging. Where can you take them next to learn more or get more interaction with you on a deeper level?

I`m always funneling people into my FB group and email list. I know that getting them in there is going to deepen their connection with me. I share content there in more detail and help people progress in their business. With that feeling of progress they get, they stick around because they want more. By doing so, the relationship with me deepens.

15. Consistency

Influence is built when you know, like, and trust with your audience. The best way to do that is consistency.

It`s no good having a spurt of motivation, showing up for a week, and then disappearing for a couple of weeks. People don`t do business with people who are flaky.

If you show up on the good and bad days and keep giving free, valuable information that gets people to take action and make progress, you will build influence with them over time.

At the end of the day, your audience wants to do business with people who are serious and stable.

Consistency = Trust
Trust = Influence

Influence is leadership.

Leadership and influence go hand in hand because effective leaders are able to exert influence over others. They possess the skills and qualities necessary to inspire trust, gain respect, and create positive change. True leadership involves more than just holding a position of authority; it requires influencing and motivating others to follow and contribute to a shared vision willingly.

Remember, building influence using video on social media takes time and consistent effort. Stay true to your brand, be authentic, and have fun with your content. With dedication, creativity, and a dash of humor, you'll build a loyal following and attract more people who want to do business with you.

Coach's Notes: In Meghan's chapter, she emphasizes the importance of visualization, repetition, clear calls to action, and consistency in building influence. One can develop trust and influence with an audience by visualizing success, repeatedly sharing core messages, providing direction, and maintaining consistent engagement. Meghan's insights underline the need for thoughtful and continuous efforts in crafting an engaging online presence, leading to business growth and personal development.

MEGHAN BRAZIER

"Overcoming self-doubt is all about believing we're enough and letting go of what the world says we're supposed to be and supposed to call ourselves."

— Brene' Brown

MELISSA L. FRITCH-GILLISPIE

- Earned five trips so far.

- Five-figure earner.

- Conqueror of being a people pleaser (except for my Mama or my Children-I`d do anything for them!)

The Hardest Struggle

We have all found ourselves in a place we never wanted to be—the depths of self-destruction, where fear and regret reign. It`s a painful existence, but within this chapter lies a revelation; Even in the midst of misery, this place can become a catalyst for a remarkable journey of personal growth.

This chapter will delve into the themes of belief, resilience, and the battles we fight against confusion, hatred, sorrow, anxiety, and depression. Throughout my time in network marketing, I have encountered countless individuals who have faced their own struggles in these areas. As we step into the spotlight of personal development, I am excited to share how you can unleash your personal transformation, tap into your limitless potential, and seize the power to rewrite your story.

I know that personally, I've spent far too long dwelling in the depths of self-destruction. Some of you probably know exactly what I am talking about. It was a place that can only be described as hell—a realm of fear, confusion, hate, regret, sorrow, madness, anxiety, and depression. There were moments when I felt so utterly lost and out of control that I feared I would never find my way back.

Part of my struggle was the labels and things I had been told about myself from a very young age. From the moment we enter this world and long into our adult lives, we're bombarded with societal messages that shape our perceptions:

- They tell us how attractive or unattractive we are.

- They categorize us as either unique or weird.

- They label us as smart or unintelligent.

- They judge our strengths or weaknesses.

- They determine our worthiness or make us feel inadequate.

The list goes on, and you can add your own statements. As innocent children, we believe what we're told, accepting these judgments as absolute truth. As teenagers, we may begin to question and feel lost, yet often fail to realize the deep-rooted damage these beliefs have caused. As we transition into adulthood, we find ourselves grappling with how to undo this so-called damage and learn to think for ourselves. You should not have to believe what you have been sold about yourself. You can break free from any label that doesn't serve you.

I found myself seeing so many things that no longer served me. I made a pivotal decision to embark on a new, better journey. I decided that I didn't want to spend a life in misery. Don't get me wrong, it was, and sometimes still is, a hard road to personal transformation that took brave action on my part. It took me deciding to do the work.

Traumas can define our past, but they don't create our future.

Fast forward to today; I dedicate myself daily to this path because it fuels my soul and drives me toward what truly matters. I've learned the power of forgiveness and granting myself grace, understanding that every step I take leads me closer to living my best life. I choose myself first, for it is only when I am at my best that I can be the best for others.

So let's circle back to you. What does it take to choose yourself first and start to make decisions based on what is best for you?

Coach's Notes: Emphasizing the ability to discard unhelpful labels and heal from trauma, Melissa underlines the importance of choosing oneself and prioritizing personal growth. She highlights that resilience and self-forgiveness can facilitate a journey toward living a more fulfilling life.

One Word can Change it All

You owe it to yourself to start by simply using this word: BELIEVE!

I'm 100% guilty of watching TV shows when I probably should be working, but there are times when you just need a means to relax and not think. I'm okay with that; we are human, after all, and not machines. One day, my hubby came home from work and mentioned a show we could watch. Now this show had been on for a while now, and I had no interest in it because it really didn't seem like it would be one for me to engage in. I was so wrong...

In the popular TV series "Ted Lasso," the main character, Ted Lasso, embodies the power of belief and its transformative impact on individuals and teams. Ted Lasso, played by Jason Sudeikis, is an American football coach who finds himself coaching a professional soccer team in England, despite having no prior experience in the sport. Throughout the series, Ted Lasso often repeats the mantra "Believe" as a guiding principle.

For Ted, "Believe" goes beyond mere optimism or blind faith. It represents a deep conviction in oneself, in the potential of others, and in the power of teamwork. Ted understands that belief is about positive thinking and cultivating a mindset that fosters resilience, perseverance, and personal growth.

By encouraging his players to believe in themselves, Ted Lasso instills newfound confidence and helps them tap into their untapped potential. He inspires them to overcome their insecurities, embrace their strengths, and strive for greatness. Ted`s unwavering belief in his team`s ability to succeed, even in the face of adversity, becomes a driving force that propels them forward.

His belief extends beyond the confines of the soccer field. He believes in the power of kindness, empathy, and genuine connections. He understands that true success lies not only in winning matches but also in nurturing relationships, fostering personal growth, and creating a positive impact on the lives of others.

Ted Lasso teaches us that belief is not just a word or a superficial concept. It is a mindset, a guiding principle that shapes our actions, relationships, and perceptions of ourselves. By embracing belief, we open ourselves up to a world of possibilities, discover our true potential, and achieve extraordinary outcomes. As Ted Lasso would say, "Believe, and you`ll be surprised at what you can achieve."

So I want you to imagine a bright yellow sign with bold blue letters that spell out "BELIEVE." It may be worn, crumpled, and torn, but let's place it right at the forefront of your mind. Secure it with black tape in each of the four corners, ensuring it's vivid and prominent in your visualization.

Now let's break down each letter and infuse it with some meaning that I feel is a good foundation for our self-belief:

B - BE BOLD: We stand firm, refusing to let others define us. Their opinions hold no power over who we truly are.

E - EFFERVESCENT: We remember our true capabilities and embrace our inner spark - our light that was born to shine for all to see.

L - LOVE: We prioritize self-love and empathy, nurturing our hearts and honoring our needs.

I - INTENTIONALLY INSPIRING: We don't seek an easy path; we pursue what is possible. Repeat after me, "Impossible = I'mPossible."

E - ELEVATE: We strive to be the best version of ourselves, rising above distractions and potential pitfalls that could derail us.

V - VIGILANT: We surround ourselves with the right people—individuals who support and guide us on our journey to greatness.

E - EVOLVE: We actively seek quality content, listening, and reading to expand our minds, preparing ourselves for growth and taking purposeful action.

Our self-beliefs shape and mold us. It is the very foundation of our personal success, which in turn strengthens our business endeavors.

We know WHO we are because our morals, values, and character define us.

We know WHAT we are capable of because we fearlessly step outside our comfort zones.

We know WHERE we belong because we choose to be in the company of those who uplift and inspire us.

We know WHEN to make decisions that impact both our personal and professional lives.

We know WHY our goals and dreams ignite a passionate fire within us. We understand they have been bestowed upon us for a reason.

The road to both failure and success is an extraordinary journey if we remain steadfast in our self-beliefs. It unveils our strengths, nurtures our confidence, reveals our boundaries, and uncovers our greatest joys. Above all, it weaves a unique story within us that is meant to be shared with the world.

As you start to believe and implement the beliefs, you are going to start to have success. The success may be big wins or small wins. I believe success comes in many forms. It`s not just about the shiny awards, impressive titles, or stacks of money. Success begins with taking deliberate and necessary steps toward living our best lives. After all, life is a magnificent journey, one that is meant to be explored and embraced.

Discovering our unique path is a mix of failures and triumphs. It involves venturing down roads less traveled, navigating detours and dead ends, and braving uncertain terrain. We evolve and grow throughout this process, constantly pushing ourselves to reach new heights. But here`s the thing: If we lack a strong mindset, we risk stagnation, forever confined to a destination of self-destruction. Trust me, that`s not where you want to be.

So, how can we embark on our journey of discovery, failure, and success without being entangled in the opinions and expectations of others? The key lies in forgiving those who unknowingly perpetuated these beliefs and dedicating ourselves to daily work on our self-belief. To believe in ourselves is to embrace our truest and most authentic form. It`s a transformative journey of self-discovery, where we shed the weight of others` expectations and step into the power of our own potential. The path to belief often means dropping those pesky opinions along the way, but it doesn`t mean we have to leave all our people behind!

Coach's Notes: Melissa urges us to believe in ourselves, using Ted Lasso's leadership as an inspiration. She breaks down "BELIEVE" into qualities like boldness, love, and evolution. Her perspective, which encourages a shift from external validation to inner fulfillment, is powerful and affirming, reminding us that success is a personal journey driven by self-belief, not societal standards.

How to Bring More Along

Once you have cultivated strong self-belief and embarked on your path of personal development, you have the incredible opportunity to bring along your favorite people—the ones who mean the most to you. Just as you have discovered the power of belief and witnessed its transformative effects in your own lives, you now have the ability to share this gift with those you hold dear.

As we continue to grow and evolve, we can extend a helping hand to our loved ones, supporting them on their own journeys of self-discovery and personal growth. By leading by example and embodying the principles we have learned, we become beacons of inspiration and encouragement to those around us.

We can create an environment that nurtures growth and fosters positivity, where open conversations, shared experiences, and meaningful connections flourish. We have the opportunity to lift others up, helping them embrace their true potential and empowering them to believe in themselves.

Through our transformation, we gain a deeper understanding of the struggles and challenges our loved ones may face. We can offer them guidance, lend a listening ear, and provide a safe space to explore their dreams and aspirations. By being present, supportive, and empathetic, we can help them navigate the twists and turns of their personal journeys.

Introducing our favorite people to valuable resources, books, podcasts, or courses that have significantly impacted our growth can be so impactful. Sharing these tools can inspire them to broaden their horizons, gain new perspectives, and continue their personal development quests.

As we journey together, we create bonds strengthened by a shared commitment to growth and self-improvement. We become a community that lifts one another up, celebrates each other`s successes, and provides a network of support through the inevitable challenges we face along the way.

Remember, however, that each person`s path is unique. While we can offer guidance and support, respecting their journeys and allowing them to find their own way is crucial. We must foster an environment where they feel free to express their authentic selves and make choices that align with their own values and aspirations.

Bringing our favorite people along on the path of self-development is a beautiful way to enrich our relationships and create a collective impact. Together, we can create a ripple effect of personal growth and empowerment that extends far beyond our immediate circles. By helping those we cherish unlock their full potential, we contribute to a world where individuals are empowered to live their best lives.

So, let us embrace the opportunity to support and uplift our favorite people as they embark on their own journeys of self-discovery. Together, we can create a community that encourages and celebrates personal growth, leaving a lasting legacy of love, inspiration, and empowerment.

This is the power of **BELIEVING!!!**

No important journey taken is complete without music. I feel music is an amazing lifeline that only upgrades our journey. So let's set the stage for your journey—a road trip of a lifetime. As you hit the open road of self-development, I want you to pick a song that means something to you. Let it be a song that can be your anthem (for me, it's "Glorious" by Macklemore, in case you're curious). Music is a powerful way of connecting with and helping us on our journey. So before you do anything else, pick your anthem - a song that speaks to you. It's okay if you need to change it a few times, but this song needs to make you feel alive; you'll know it when it does.

Put that song on and listen. Really listen and absorb every moment, allowing the music to fill your senses. Play it loud to invigorate your spirit or softly to savor the lyrics. Dance to the rhythm or stand still, soaking in the melodies. Sing along or simply listen, allowing the music to stir your soul. Let it guide you to new destinations, especially those scenic routes you've only dreamed of. Embrace the liberating feeling that accompanies this journey. Your anthem is now part of your journey. When you find yourself doubting or feeling down, play your anthem! It will remind you of how important you and your journey really are!

Don`t forget to take your favorite people along. Life is so much more rewarding when we can share our experiences together.

Make it fun, make it memorable, make it LEGENDARY!!!

Melissa L. Fritch-Gillispie
Your Friend and Fellow Self-Believer

Coach's Notes: As a trusted friend and seasoned mastermind participant, Melissa reminds us of the strength found in collective growth. Her message beautifully marries individual journeys with communal empowerment, suggesting the emotional power of a personal anthem. Through her heartfelt words, she draws a vivid image of a supportive community, underlining the importance of shared experiences on the path to self-discovery.

*"The meaning of life is
to find your gift.
The purpose of life is
to give it away."*

— Pablo Picasso

PAULA WEEKS

- Nine years in the industry.

- Achieved number one power rank within the country.

- Achieved top earner within the country.

- Serves on The Wellness Council for the company.

- Serves on the Partners Council for the company.

What is "Taprooting" within Network Marketing?

Taprooting is the process of connecting to your network with the intention of connecting them to your product or service at some stage and then repeating this process by connecting through your network into their network and so on.

So if this is what taprooting is, then what do I think authentic taprooting is?

I believe in connecting with people to genuinely help them. Not to sell them a product or sign them up for my business. Our industry already has a bad enough reputation for being worse than dodgy car salespeople without adding to that by being "pushy scam artists." By shifting your focus to seeing each person as an individual who has an individual set of needs which you may be able to help them with at some point in their life, means that this is what people will "feel" from you rather than that icky and urgent feel you can give off when you`re just trying to sell them whatever your company offers, even if they may not need it!

Coach's Notes: Paula's noteworthy industry experience fortifies her insights on taprooting. Her focus on authentic connections over immediate sales exemplifies the essence of building lasting relationships in network marketing.

An opportunity to help them may not be present straight away. But eventually, the opportunity to help in any way, not just by offering your products or business opportunity, will present itself. I`ve done a lot of training and personal development in network marketing and have been told by a few trainers and top leaders that being a "connector" of people and services to genuinely help others will always come back to repay you. Authentically connect people in your network with other products and services (not necessarily from your company) that can help them and will then return the same favor to you when someone in your network needs your products and services. Help others without the expectation of it in return, and it really will come back to you!

Since I joined this industry almost nine years ago, authentic taprooting has been the single biggest skill I have used to build a successful, six figure residual business. I am naturally an introvert. Meaning I still like to be around people and interact in small groups of people, but when I`m done peopling, I need to retreat to silence and solitude to recharge. I tell you this so that if you are the same, you`ll know by the end of this chapter that you can also build a successful business in network marketing.

Sometimes it`s hard to find your way in this business because the extroverts of the world show up bold and bright, like beacons of flashing light, that everyone can`t help but notice, but we introvert who want to find our own quiet, consistent and most of all, authentic way to be successful, can absolutely do it. I am proof of that.

I don`t like the spotlight, although I`m ok with speaking at company events on the stage in front of big crowds because I love to educate and bring value to people. I`m really passionate about helping others in lots of aspects but in particular with their health. My twenty years as a Registered Nurse means I lead with this, which makes things really simple. Over time people learn that you really care about helping people rather than selling them products. When they`ve eventually seen enough "exposure" to your product or service and need it in their life, they will reach out to you because they "know, like, and trust" you. It`s at this point that authentic taprooting can begin. Building authentic relationships that bring value to your life is really important. Make sure the people who surround you are "your" people so that you feel supported to be your authentic self; when you`re your authentic self, it`s easier to taproot authentically.

When you make sales to your network, excellent customer service is a top priority, especially when using taprooting, for the following reasons:

1. So you can get repeat customers from them.

2. To build a brand that people trust.

3. Happy customers sometimes become happy brand partners.

4. Because happy customers naturally talk to their network, and if they don`t want to "do the business," you want them to recommend YOU as the go-to person.

One phrase I use a lot when taprooting into other people`s networks, because let`s be honest, not everyone wants to do this business but is still happy to make recommendations, is:

"I don`t know if you know, but my business is built on recommendations and referrals, so I would really appreciate it if you see someone in your network who could use my products that you would put my name forward to them for me."

This statement has led me to many, many customers and brand partners as well. When I`m out and about in normal everyday life, I look for opportunities to assist the person in front of me or their network because most people have stuff going on in their life that they need help with. It helps to be a good listener and care about other people`s issues. This can be tiring and overwhelming at times, so it`s important that you have boundaries (for everyone`s benefit). From Rob Sperry himself at an event in Melbourne back in 2018, I learned the skill of being a "giver" with boundaries.

Another way I have taprooted into other people`s networks is by connecting over social media when you`re in person with someone. This feels much more "normal" than connecting after the fact because people move on with their lives pretty quickly, and you can be forgotten easily.

When I first started in this business, we did many in-home presentations and get-togethers. Clearly, this was pre-covid! We would ask our friends or new teammates to host a get-together where they would invite their network to see a short presentation relating to our products. At that presentation, we would then network with everyone afterward and connect individually. Most people would either have questions, purchase something, or need extra information that we might need to get to them later down the track in the days after the presentation.

So we would find each other on Facebook and "friend" each other and send a short message in Messenger (whilst in front of them) to prompt us as to why we had set up the message. For example, "Hey, Milly, great to connect with you here at Gemma`s house. I`ll chase up that information you wanted about XYZ". That way, we knew why we were connected and messaging each other. I don`t know how many times I, now nine years later, still rely on those short messages to prompt me as to how I am connected to that person from all those years before. These people may or may not purchase from you on the night, months, or years afterward, but you are connected on Facebook, meaning they see your posts and get to "know" you over social media.

People are always watching. Whether or not they like or comment on your posts, they are watching. You never know what will eventually lead them to reach out for help with your products or services. Oftentimes those people will tag their network in my posts on Facebook when they see something that relates to their network (most likely because I`ve used the phrase above and they want to help me out or because they really think their friend might need the product or service I`m offering). This is an opportunity to connect with them. I always click on that person`s profile and send them a message that might say something along the lines of "Hey Lee, your friend Tracey tagged you in my post I did last night on my profile. Are you needing help with .......? I could send you a fact sheet on it if that would help?". If they reply, I`ll send them a friend request, so I`m also connected to their network. People don`t always reply, and that`s ok.

Another way to taproot using social media is to invite people to tag their friends in a post on my profile (which is set to public so that anyone can see it). It`s human nature that people like to talk about themselves and/or share their opinion. I don`t like to be too controversial, but you can choose a topic that is trending and invite people to discuss it via your post. I like to choose funny, slightly obscure topics that give people a laugh because laughter is the best medicine! I might add to the post, "Tag a friend below who would agree." The best outcome from this would be to have people laugh and connect with each other and a new person connect with me via the post because they relate to my content and find it entertaining. When people relate and feel connected, they might send me a friend request or follow me (which means they still see my content). By choosing content showcasing you and your personality, you will draw like-minded people to you, and working with like-minded people is fun and easier for introverts!

Coach's Notes: As a fellow introvert, I resonate with Paula's experience. She proves that introverts can excel in network marketing by using their unique qualities for genuine engagement. Her empathetic approach is a testament to our industry's power of authentic connections.

Make sure to publicly share your true personality and vision or "why" on social media and in personal conversation so that people can connect with you and feel your authenticity. There's no point in spouting how authentic and real you are but then showing the opposite behavior in a person with someone or even online on social media. I see people posting one thing, being negative, and whinging the next minute. If you confuse your audience, they won't know what to expect from you and won't feel confident buying from you.

One way I've seen multiple brand reps in many different companies taproot via social media is by asking your friends, family, and customers to post on their social media about their experience using your products or services and tag you in the post, directing their audience to connect directly with you for information about the products or services. For example, I've asked people to write up a short testimony on the product they have used and loved so that we can post it in our shared testimony group on Facebook. This is a group that our whole team uses as a tool to build their business. It`s where we all add our interested people and tag them in a testimonial or info post related to the information they want about a particular product. In adding them, it also means they then have access to seeing all the other products that we have in our range. Sometimes people can be in the group for years before they make a decision to buy. As well as asking them to post it in our testimony group, sometimes I also ask them if they are willing to post it on their personal profile and tag me in it so that their network can see it.

Their network knows, likes, and trusts them, and if they personally recommend me, that trust usually extends to me. This is a great way to get people who want to help you but don`t want to do business to share their network with you. How many times have you heard from people that the reason why they don`t want to do the business is that they don`t want to pester their friends and family, but when you offer them this option because you`re the one technically financially benefiting from the potential sales, they are ok with it! Of course, if this option goes particularly well, then I`ll have the conversation with a person that if they want to join first, then all the people who have commented and want to purchase could be their first customers or potential brand partners. Sometimes people opt to take it on; sometimes, they don`t. Either way, you have successfully taprooted into someone else network, and that`s always a good thing as it keeps your business moving forward.

Coach's Notes: Paula cleverly leverages customers' trust to extend her reach. Her strategy of letting customers' endorsements vouch for her products and services showcases thoughtful and sincere marketing.

"It's about using the right tools, with the right triggers within a proper marketing framework."

— Vishen Lakhiani

SARAH BJORGAARD

- 32 Years in Network Marketing.

- Voted one of Utah`s 30 Women to Watch.

- Winner of the Silver Stevie Award for Lifetime Achievement in Network Marketing.

- Has Built a Multi-Million dollar record breaking team with over 50,000 members in under two years!

- Holds Top Rank of Presidential Diamond.

The day Dulcie joined my team was the definition of exhilarating! She was looking for a solution to challenges she was personally experiencing. but she was also looking for something new career-wise to inspire her again. She was burnt out and just not feeling the passion she had once felt. This seemed to be a perfect fit in all ways, and her excitement and her dreams made me 'born again' in the opportunity. With the responsibility I felt to help her achieve her goals, I was firmly committed at that moment to make sure that I took her on the journey that would best support her success!

Getting new customers or business builders started on their journey is one of the most exciting times in your business. It feels like watching a child take their first steps, graduate from high school, or even watching them get married.

Every customer starts using your product because they believe that the product you advertise will make a difference for them in some way. They connected with you, your story, and your passion around what you offer. Their hope is at an all-time high because they need a solution to a problem. What`s important to understand is that they generally do not enroll because of the company or company advertising. Again, they enrolled because of you!

Every business builder has the same hope and desire as a customer but also sees the vision of their life if they succeed like you.

Coach's Notes: Sarah's focus on the individual's journey — customers or business builders — really hits home. It's crucial to remember that every person who joins your team comes with their own hopes and desires, and it's our job to help them actualize those dreams.

Both customers and business builders need to be taken on a communication journey that will make all the difference in their results, their beliefs, and, most importantly, their retention.

In the six companies that I have worked for and been around the boardroom table or been in the field, the one consistency that I see is a customer or business builder dropping off the radar after the first or second purchase. Generally, if they purchase for ninety days consistently, you have a much better chance of them sticking with you, and if you can get them to the fourth month, it can be transformative for them personally and for your business.

How you onboard your new customer or business builder determines how many you have that pass ninety days and reach the fourth month and beyond.

I`m not perfect, and I`ve certainly made mistakes along the way, but every new customer and every new business builder has allowed me to shape and shift what I believe is the best version of what my onboarding looks like today. The same will be true for you.

There are a few principles that every business builder should know as you grow your team. There are processes you can use to help you develop your systems. Finally, there are platforms to help you scale.

In the next few pages, we will discuss the principles, processes, and platforms to help you successfully onboard new customers and new business builders. Let`s get started!

The Principles

"The reason why principles are so important is that principles make life (business) predictable."

— Mules Munroe

1. Start small & follow who`s gone before you.

2. Everything you do duplicates.

3. Systemize your onboarding.

4. While building momentum, get set up for the next phase of growth.

5. Begin to scale and automate your systems.

Coach's Notes: This is an essential takeaway. As your team grows, so does the need to automate processes like onboarding. Automated systems ensure consistency, freeing up your time to focus on nurturing relationships and developing new strategies.

Start Small

When you are just beginning your business, it`s important to lean into the systems that your upline or those that have gone before you use. They have been where you are and have gone through all of the phases in this chapter. Hundreds or thousands have used the same training to become successful, break records, and reach their goals.

If you do not have strong support teams who have gone before you, grab a notebook and jot down the things you would want to know when you were getting your business started. It will be easy to share what you`ve written down with a phone call or two. Just remember, this doesn`t have to be fancy. It`s about taking your newest customer or newest business builder on a journey.

Everything You Do Duplicates

This is a big one, and sometimes we fail to understand that it works for both good and not-so-good. As humans, we tend to replicate what we see others do. You`ve heard the old cliché, monkey see, monkey do. In other words, what you demonstrate, and what you do, others will watch and begin to duplicate within their own teams. That`s true for all things about network marketing, especially onboarding. You want to keep things simple and systematic so that your team stays in momentum.

Systemize Your Onboarding

As you begin moving up in the business, you will refine what works for you, and your team likely will be using what your enroller or upline had as a base. It`s the same process all successful people have used on their journey; we all start somewhere!

Whether you are working with a customer or a business builder, knowing what you do and when you do it is important.

When I was just beginning, I put together a very simple spreadsheet that left room for the name of the person on the left-hand side and the steps I followed along the top. Every time I completed a step with each person, I checked it off or wrote the date. Over time, I found steps that I didn`t need, I consistently missed, or I needed to add. After a good run of new enrollments, I felt like I had a pretty baked process that was working to support my new customers and business builders.

While Building Momentum, Get Set Up for the Next Phase of Success

No business is ever in momentum forever. In network marketing, you are either in momentum and holding on for your life, or you are building momentum for your next phase of growth. Both places are good places! Momentum is fun, inspiring, out of control, results-driven, and full of vision! Building momentum is more methodical, reflective, and intentional and a time to prepare for your next big wave of growth! Take the time to reflect on what has worked, what isn`t working, and what you need to tweak, implement, or change. You`ve been gifted this time for preparation! Remember, "You can`t get from mountain top to mountain top without going through the valleys, and the valleys are where you get good."

Begin to Scale and Automate Your Systems

As you begin your business and move up within your compensation plan, you may need to automate your onboarding for customers and business builders based on momentum or size. Automation allows you time to step away from the business and be present. It also solidifies that everyone gets the same kind of messaging out of the gate. Some companies will allow you to have an API in their system. If your company does allow this – I highly recommend it as no one falls through the cracks.

The Process

"Focus on the process, and the results will come."

– #gymaholic

As mentioned in our **Principle – Systemize Your Onboarding**, it's important to begin small, craft your process, and refine it over time. I call it "journey mapping." You are writing out <u>what</u> should be communicated and <u>when</u> for each segmentation. If you started when your team was smaller with the notebook or the spreadsheet approach, you likely have a jump start.

Customers and business partners will both need different journey maps. Customers will be heavier on satisfaction, product education, company programs like auto-ship, or even referral marketing opportunities.

Business builders will be heavier on goal setting, programs to earn money out of the gate, rank benefits, connecting with the community, events, and product education.

I recommend starting to craft your process or system with the segmentation that you enroll the most. If you enroll mostly customers, having a process in place to onboard your customers will be critical, and the same goes for your business builders if that`s where you lean.

Let's Start with Customers

As a consumer of your product, ask yourself what is critical for a new customer to know. On our team, we personally have ten touchpoints over the first ninety days. Here is an example of those touch points that might give you a place to start if you are beginning from scratch:

1. Welcome (upon enrollment)

2. Unboxing Day (when the product arrives)

3. First Product Experience

4. 1 Week on the Product

5. 2 Weeks on the Product

6. 3 Weeks on the Product

7. 4 Weeks on the Product

8. 8 Weeks on the Product

9. 12 Weeks on the Product

10. Bonus Message

Each message is generic enough to appear to be written by the enroller. They discuss different programs and incentives that are pertinent during their customer journey. The bonus message allows them to receive a link for additional product resources in case they need them at any time!

If you are easily overwhelmed, just write one message at a time as it needs to be written. Over a three-month period, you will have an official system in place that can be tweaked or changed at any time.

Next, let's Talk About Business Builders

This segmentation of your business will be more progressive. Business builders will need to "launch" their business in this process, and it will also need to provide a level of support and inspiration along the way!

Typically, this launch process or system will last approximately five weeks for our organization.

Here is a sample of how we support our business builders. Of course, every business and every company is different, so this might just give you a base to begin with.

1. Welcome to the Team

2. Getting Started – Series of 3 Steps

3. Preparing to Launch – Series of 8 Steps

4. Launching Your Business – Series of 8 Steps

5. Growing Your Network – Series of 22 Steps

6. Bonus Social Media Workshop – Series of 6 Steps

Coach's Notes: I love how Sarah stresses breaking the process down into bite-sized steps. In network marketing, overwhelming your new business builders is a common pitfall. Keeping things manageable and digestible can truly make a difference in their success.

Each of the six messages is broken down into bite sized pieces or steps. Most can be accomplished quickly, but we`ve found that each step allows people to feel more accomplished and like they are making progress. Launching your business and growing your network lasts approximately 28 days. They essentially give the new business builder exactly what to do daily from a social marketing standpoint.

Like the customer message, each of these messages and steps can be written as you need them rather than all at once.

The Platforms

Utilizing platforms to scale your business along the way will allow you to both step away and be present at the same time!

During the early stages of our growth as a team, we utilized a team page with each of our onboarding steps for business builders in guides. Leaders would tag their new people in the welcome message and follow along their journey with them.

Over time, as our team`s momentum grew, and we reached 500,000, 1,000,000, and 2,000,000+ in organizational volume monthly, it was evident that we needed to automate our onboarding to ensure that new customers and new business builders were not falling through the cracks. Automating your onboarding allows you to be sure that everyone is receiving consistent messaging.

For both our customer and our business builder onboarding, our builders will send the initial welcome message. Then the new customer or builder is prompted to text a keyword to our team text service, and from there, they will be added to a drip campaign where on specific days, the appropriate messages will be texted right to their phone!

If you are overwhelmed hearing this, know it took us about 1.5 years to implement it. This certainly wasn`t overnight; it took some thought and strategy to nail the messages! I cannot stress enough to start small. Build on what`s working for you as you move along your journey!

"Dulcie has been an unbelievable success story from someone who started with a true need to someone who caught the vision of where she wanted to go. She's brought an incredible impact on her family! Much of this was uncovered & nurtured along the way during her onboarding process."

Remember that our job as leaders is to do one thing really well; paint the picture, and help others see themselves in it. If you do this every step of the way during your onboarding process, there is no telling the level of success you will achieve and the number of people you will help.

*"All our dreams can come true,
if we have the courage to pursue them."*

— Walt Disney

SEAN SMITH

- Built an Organization of over 5,000 recurring customers.

- Created an organization of over $125,000 in recurring commissionable billing revenue in thirty months.

- Coached and mentored a diverse organization that expands the continental U.S. & Canada.

Unleashing the Power of Network Marketing – It's a Process, Not an Event

Welcome, my friends, to the exhilarating world of network marketing. If you find yourself here, it means you`re ready to dive into this incredible industry and embark on a journey that can transform your life. So, fasten your seatbelts and get ready for some empowering insights that will ignite your network marketing career like never before.

Network marketing isn`t a quick fix or a one-time event; it`s a step-by-step process. In this chapter, we will unveil the key ingredients to help you find success in this game-changing business model.

Recruiting: The Art of Building a Powerful Team

I`m about to unleash the secrets to recruiting like a true champion. Are you ready to take your team to new heights? Are you hungry for success and eager to make a game-changing difference in your life? Well, buckle up because recruiting is not for the faint-hearted. It`s an art that demands effort, persistence, and top-notch communication skills.

Picture this: a team of unstoppable go-getters, each possessing a burning passion to excel in their field. These are the individuals who challenge the status quo, who push boundaries, and who never settle for mediocrity. They`re the ones who will transform your team into a force to be reckoned with. Imagine the exhilaration of curating a diverse roster where everyone brings their unique talents and fuels the collective power. Together, you become an unstoppable powerhouse, achieving greatness that goes beyond anything you`ve ever imagined.

But here`s the deal—effective recruiting starts with explosive communication. It`s about fostering an environment where bold ideas are shared, debated, and transformed into groundbreaking innovations. Open dialogue becomes the norm, and constructive feedback flows freely to drive continuous improvement. As a leader, you must master the art of listening, tuning in to understand the perspectives of others, and inspiring them with your vision. It`s through your magnetic communication skills that trust is built, and your team becomes an unstoppable force, ready to conquer any challenge that comes your way.

Now, buckle up and get ready for the ride of your life. Building a powerful team is not just a destination; it`s an epic journey of growth and transformation. You hold the key to unlocking the hidden potential within your team members and propelling them toward leadership roles that will shape your organization`s future. Celebrate their victories, fuel their ambition, and empower them to take ownership of their roles. With your guidance, they`ll flourish into leaders who can ignite the world around them.

So the time has come to take action. Step into the realm of recruiting like the champion you are, seeking out those extraordinary individuals who hunger for success and are ready to make a game-changing difference. Embrace explosive communication, where ideas flow freely and trust takes root. Invest in the growth and development of your team, propelling them toward greatness. Let`s embark on this thrilling adventure fueled by the passion and drive that will set your team apart from the rest. Get ready to recruit like a true champion – the world awaits your unstoppable power!

Action Steps:

1. Learn to become a professional inviter!

2. Continue to Show the Plan

3. The Fortune is in the Follow Up

4. Invite To The Next Event

Coach's Notes: Sean nails this by emphasizing the importance of recruitment in building a successful network marketing team. Remember that recruitment isn't just about numbers; quality should be your ultimate goal. Aim to recruit those who share the same vision and drive and bring diversity to your team. Different backgrounds, experiences, and perspectives can fuel innovation and resilience within your team. Also, while communication is key in recruitment, don't forget the power of leading by example. Show your team your work ethic, passion, and commitment to the business. This way, you set the standard and inspire them to follow suit.

Customer Acquisition: Building Lifelong Connections

Get ready because we`re about to embark on a thrilling journey of customer acquisition that will leave you hungry for success and ready to take action! Picture this: a rock-solid product or service that blows minds, leaving customers in awe of its transformative power. To excel in this realm, you must immerse yourself in the intricacies of what you`re offering, understanding its value inside and out. Learn everything you can about it, become an expert, and ignite the belief in potential customers that this is exactly what they need to revolutionize their lives.

But here`s the secret ingredient – customer acquisition is not just about making a sale; it`s about cultivating lifelong connections. Approach this task with empathy, genuine care, and a mindset of service. Dive deep into your customer`s world, listen attentively to their needs, and empathize with their pain points. By truly understanding their desires and challenges, you can offer tailored solutions that resonate with them on a deeper level. Your goal is to provide real value, setting yourself apart as a trustworthy authority in the industry and ensuring their success becomes your top priority.

To achieve customer acquisition mastery, you must harness effective communication power. Picture this: your messaging is crystal clear, concise, and relatable, avoiding any complicated jargon or technical terms that might alienate potential customers. Instead, you speak their language, addressing their concerns directly and authentically. Every interaction is built on a foundation of trust as you consistently deliver on your promises, surpassing their expectations time and time again. Through these authentic connections, loyalty is born, transforming customers into loyal advocates for your brand and active participants in its growth.

Keep in mind that in the realm of network marketing, no one gets paid unless customers are gathered. The key to achieving success lies in building lasting relationships founded on trust, value, and genuine care for your customer`s success. Establish yourself as a go-to resource, a beacon of knowledge and support that they can rely on. Nurture these connections, going above and beyond to ensure their needs are met and exceeded. By doing so, you secure their long-term loyalty and unlock the powerful potential of word-of-mouth advertising as they excitedly share their positive experiences with others.

Are you ready to take action? The realm of customer acquisition awaits your passion and dedication. Step into this domain with a burning desire to create lifelong connections. Educate yourself about your product or service, understanding its value inside and out. Cultivate genuine relationships based on trust and value, and approach each interaction with empathy and a mindset of service. Communicate with clarity and authenticity, fostering trust and exceeding expectations at every turn. Remember, customer acquisition is not just about making sales; it`s about building a community of loyal advocates who will propel your brand to new heights. The time has come to unleash your potential, conquer challenges, and embark on this exhilarating journey of customer acquisition mastery!

Action Steps:

1. Become your own customer and be an ambassador for your own product or service.

2. Acquire customers from individuals that have said no to your opportunity.

Coach's Notes: The focus on building long-term relationships is spot on! It's not just about making a sale but creating a connection. Customer acquisition also requires understanding your ideal customer. As you learn more about your product, spend some time

defining who your ideal customer is. What are their interests? What challenges are they facing that your product can solve? A clear picture of who you're trying to reach can make your sales and marketing efforts more effective.

Networking: Expand Your Circle

The world of network marketing is an exciting and ever-evolving industry that thrives on the power of connections. Whether you`re a seasoned professional or just starting out, one thing is certain; networking is everything. It is the lifeblood of success in this industry, and it`s time for you to take action and harness its immense potential.

In today`s digital age, online networking has revolutionized how we connect. Platforms like social media, online forums, and virtual communities have opened up endless possibilities for expanding your circle. Imagine the thrill of engaging in conversations with like-minded individuals who share your passion and drive. Picture yourself connecting with industry influencers who have already paved the way to success. Envision the limitless potential of reaching out to potential prospects who could become loyal customers or valuable team members.

But online networking is more than just creating profiles or posting content. It`s about actively participating in meaningful conversations, sharing valuable insights, and showcasing your expertise. It`s about building relationships, one interaction at a time. So, dive into relevant groups or communities, contribute thoughtfully, and let your unique voice be heard. With every comment, every share, and every connection request, you are broadening your reach and establishing your authority in the network marketing world.

While online networking is undoubtedly powerful, don`t underestimate the magic of offline connections. The art of face-to-face interaction is still alive and thriving. Imagine attending events, conferences, and seminars related to your industry, where you can meet people who are just as passionate as you are. Picture yourself engaging in genuine conversations, listening attentively to the stories and experiences shared by those who have walked the path before you. Visualize the opportunities for collaboration and learning that await you in the realm of offline networking.

In-person networking allows for a deeper level of engagement. It enables you to forge relationships built on trust and genuine connection. When you meet someone face-to-face, you can truly understand their needs and aspirations. You can offer support, provide valuable insights, and be generous with your time and knowledge. By doing so, you become more than just a network marketer; you become a trusted advisor, a friend, and a mentor. It is these authentic connections that will propel you toward success in the long run.

Networking is not about selling or pushing products but building relationships and delivering value. It`s about genuinely caring for others and helping them achieve their goals. Imagine adopting a mindset of service and collaboration, where every interaction is an opportunity to make a positive impact. Visualize yourself being an active listener, truly seeking to understand the challenges and aspirations of those you engage with. Envision the joy of sharing relevant insights, offering support, and witnessing firsthand the transformation that occurs when you uplift others.

By approaching networking with this mindset, you create a strong and supportive network of individuals who truly appreciate your genuine approach. They are not just customers or business contacts but allies, cheerleaders, and partners on your journey to success. These are the people who will refer prospects to you, promote your products or services, and celebrate your victories. They are the foundation upon which your network marketing empire will be built.

Now is the time to act. Embrace the power of networking, both online and offline. Attend events, join communities, and seek out mentors who can guide you on your path to greatness. Engage in conversations, share valuable content, and actively participate in relevant groups or communities online. But don`t stop there. Step outside your comfort zone and attend industry-related events, conferences, and seminars in person. Forge genuine connections, listen attentively, and seize opportunities for collaboration and growth.

Remember, networking is not merely a means to an end; it is a lifelong journey filled with excitement, growth, and transformative experiences. So, act today and become part of a vibrant Network Marketing community. Embrace the possibilities, cultivate meaningful connections, and unleash your true potential in this dynamic industry. The future is yours for the taking.

Actionable Item:

Meet at least five new people daily, whether online or offline. Make this a core component of your DNA and daily method of operation (DMO).

Coach's Notes: Networking is crucial in this industry, and Sean has highlighted this point brilliantly. I'd add to remember to be genuine in your interactions. People appreciate sincerity and can often sense when someone is being disingenuous. Whether you're connecting with a potential customer or a new team member, always show genuine interest in the person. This builds trust and encourages more open and honest communication!

Personal Growth

Imagine the excitement of immersing yourself in a world of endless personal growth opportunities. Visualize the transformation that awaits as you invest in yourself, expanding your knowledge, skills, and mindset. The network marketing industry is your playground for self-improvement, and it`s time to take action and supercharge your success.

Education is the key that unlocks the doors to greatness in network marketing. Immerse yourself in educational resources that provide valuable insights into the industry. Dive into books, podcasts, webinars, and online courses that offer practical tips, expert advice, and proven strategies. Surround yourself with the knowledge that propels you forward and equips you with the tools needed to thrive. With each piece of wisdom you absorb, you become more empowered and unstoppable on your journey.

But personal growth extends beyond just acquiring information. It`s about inner transformation and cultivating a mindset of success. Develop an unwavering belief in yourself and your abilities. Visualize your goals and dreams, affirming your own worthiness and potential. It`s time to shed self-doubt and embrace the power within you. Surround yourself with positive influences, whether through reading inspiring books or engaging with uplifting individuals. Attend seminars and workshops where you can connect with like-minded individuals and tap into a sea of collective wisdom. By investing in personal development, you elevate not only your confidence levels but also your overall well-being.

In network marketing, adaptability is essential. The industry is constantly evolving, with new trends and strategies emerging. Stay ahead of the curve by staying updated with industry trends and adopting a mindset of constant improvement. Take advantage of training resources provided by reputable companies and industry leaders. Seek out mentorship programs that provide guidance and support from seasoned professionals who have already paved the way to success. Don`t forget the power of online courses, where you can learn at your own pace and gain valuable insights from experts around the world. Commit to lifelong learning as a key component of your success strategy, ensuring you are equipped with the latest skills and techniques that set you apart from the competition.

But personal growth is not limited to just knowledge and skills. It encompasses all aspects of your life, including your physical and mental well-being. Take care of yourself holistically, ensuring you have the energy and mental clarity needed to thrive in network marketing. Prioritize exercise, healthy eating, and self-care practices that nourish your body and mind. When you prioritize your well-being, you show up as your best self, ready to take on any challenge that comes your way.

In network marketing, success is not simply about selling products or building a team but personal transformation and becoming the best version of yourself. By investing in your own growth, you position yourself for limitless success and fulfillment. Imagine the joy of waking up every day, excited about the opportunities that lie ahead. Picture yourself confidently navigating the challenges and obstacles, knowing that you have the knowledge and skills to overcome them. Envision the life you desire, where financial freedom and personal fulfillment co-exist harmoniously.

It`s time to take action and embark on a journey of self-discovery and growth. Challenge yourself to push beyond your comfort zone, embracing new opportunities and experiences. Seek out the resources and support systems that will propel you forward on your path to success. With each step you take towards personal growth, you become a beacon of inspiration for others, igniting a ripple effect of transformation within the network marketing community.

The time is now. Invest in yourself, cultivate personal growth, and witness the magic that unfolds in your network marketing journey.

Embrace the possibilities, adopt a mindset of constant improvement, and believe in your own limitless potential. The power to create the life of your dreams is within your grasp. Seize it with both hands and embark on a transformative journey toward network marketing greatness. Your future awaits.

Action Step: Spend: 20-30 minutes every day on personal development. It can be listening to a motivational podcast. Listening to an Audiobook or reading a chapter in a personal growth book.

"Don't wait to get ready,

to get ready."

— Les Brown

STEFANO ORRU

- Top 7 in earnings worldwide in company.

- Produced 200 million dollars in sales volume in the last four years.

- Made over 3.5 million dollar in profit.

- Built everything on social media.

- Over 150,000 customer orders every year.

Attracting Customers Through Personal Brand & Social Media

I joined network marketing and direct sales in 2012. I found my path in this business due to the potential for exponential growth, leverage, and learning. The idea of aiding others to reach their objectives while simultaneously achieving my own was deeply appealing. Despite my lack of experience in marketing, business, team building, or communication, I saw something in this system that resonated with me.

I saw it working. I had been introduced to this business by a trusted friend of my father. His recommendation carried weight and gave me the confidence to embark on this new journey.

My decision to take this leap was fueled by a growing dissatisfaction with my life at the time. I was a student pursuing psychology without real conviction, as it was more a product of directionless drifting than a true passion. Although I never earned a degree, I invested substantial time in studying. On top of this, I was working part-time, three to four days a week as a waiter in a pizzeria. I was stuck in a rut and was more than ready for a change when this business opportunity came along.

My life took a transformative turn when I chanced upon a book by Tony Robbins. Reading it was akin to sowing a seed of belief in my mind — it reinforced my conviction that I could elevate my standards and achieve anything I set my mind to. This newfound perspective triggered a quest within me, a search for something more meaningful, more fulfilling.

My search, as if guided by fate, led me to the right people who introduced me to the world of network marketing. That's how my journey began, marked by a book and spurred by an insatiable desire for change.

My excitement was palpable at the onset of my venture into network marketing. I immediately reached out to my family, particularly my brother, making grand claims about becoming millionaires through this new endeavor. My enthusiasm, however, was tinged with naivety — I didn't fully comprehend the system yet was utterly convinced of our impending success.

Coach's Notes: Stefano shared how he jumped headfirst into network marketing with little experience. It's a great example of why we love this business so much! You don't have to be an expert to start. So if you find yourself giving excuses that you aren't ready, remember

that you don't need to be. If you are just starting out and not having booming success, don't be discouraged if things don't work out immediately. Persistence and willingness to learn are key in this industry.

In truth, entering this field without any skills or competence, devoid of any understanding of what was required, and with no established system to guide us was challenging. We were trying to make headway using offline methods, hosting parties and hotel meetings, pitching to people, and relentlessly contacting our friends and family. But our approach fell flat — it simply didn`t work the way we had envisioned.

In retrospect, I can see clearly that my initial attempts were misguided. I was not navigating the landscape of network marketing effectively, and my approach needed substantial refinement. I was trying to sprint before learning to walk, and this mismatch between my expectations and reality was a sobering lesson in the nuances of network marketing.

I consider myself fortunate because my sponsor, at that time, had already accumulated two decades of experience in this business. He gave me sound advice—while he understood the ins and outs of running the business offline, he also recognized the need to pivot online. We knew that people were increasingly congregating on Facebook, which boasted a staggering user base of 600 million in 2012—an important statistic that will make more sense as my story unfolds. The majority of these users, however, were yet to fully grasp how to harness the platform effectively.

Fast forward to the end of 2013, nearly seventeen months later, my venture had made no progress—zero sales, zero team partners, just a complete blank slate. Not even my mother had bought a single product, despite me having invested my own money into procuring products for both myself and my family.

Undeterred by this setback, my sponsor encouraged me, saying, "Let`s find a way. Let`s venture into another industry. Let`s invest in some courses." The challenge, however, lay in the fact that no specific courses on social media, specifically tailored for network marketing, were available at that time. Of course, the landscape has evolved, and many experts offer insight into leveraging social media in our industry. But back then, we were largely on our own, navigating this new terrain with limited guidance.

We found inspiration in a group of young individuals from the UK who were part of our same company. They were successfully acquiring customers on Facebook, a feat we were eager to replicate but didn`t quite understand how. So, we turned to espionage — studying their methods, examining their tactics, trying to decipher their strategy.

While we didn`t discover their exact approach, we managed to piece together our own interpretation. We thought, "If they`re doing this, we can emulate it in our own way." Our strategy involved building a group, populating it with testimonials, and inviting people to join.

Once we initiated the invitation process, we realized that the questions from interested individuals were often repetitive. This led us to develop a concise script, a pre-prepared list of question-answer pairs to help overcome objections. Our method of communication was rudimentary — simply copying and pasting the text, as audio and video messages were not an option at the time. Nonetheless, this strategy led to us signing our first customer online.

Around this time, we were invited to Miami by my sponsor. He opened his home to me and my brother, despite our lack of visible success, our business was still not generating any revenue. Perhaps he saw something in us, and believed in our potential more than we did ourselves. His belief in us was unequivocal, and that made all the difference.

Coach's Notes: That first sale was a significant milestone for Stefano! Remember, it's often the small wins that lead to big successes. Never underestimate the power of starting small and scaling up. Keep going!

Our first online customer was based in Italy, a sale made while we were in Miami. In this new model, we didn`t handle the products directly, the company shipped the product, and our role was solely to generate leads and convert them. All we had to do was ask for their details and provide a link, given the shift in circumstances now. The customer would then make a purchase through an e-commerce site, and we would earn a commission.

I distinctly remember the date; The 26th of December 2013 when we secured our first customer. We exchanged a look of understanding and excitement. This single sale, a modest $160 worth of product, may not have seemed like much, but to us, it was the spark that ignited our belief. The belief that if we could make one sale, we could make millions more in the following ten years using our system.

Our system, which I`ll detail more in a moment, wasn`t just ours alone. It was shared with many others, including my sponsor. As we began to see its potential, we gave our collective efforts a name, forging a sense of identity and unity. We dubbed ourselves the "Unstoppable Generation," christening our community in 2014. Along with the name, we fostered a distinct culture within our community, a culture defined by shared values, a common vision, and an unshakeable belief in our system.

With a shared vision, principles, and values, we nurtured our community and watched our business soar to unimaginable heights. To date, we`ve generated over $600 million in product sales for two companies, having transitioned to a new company four years ago.

In terms of customers, we`ve acquired somewhere between 2.5 to 3 million—and that`s a conservative estimate.

Initially, our business model was predicated on high-value customers— fewer in number but with higher average spending. Today, our approach has evolved somewhat. We sell more products to a broader customer base, yet our overall sales revenue remains impressive, exceeding $600 million.

Currently, our business generates over $50 million in sales volume per year. Each month, we add 15,000 to 20,000 new customers and recruit 1,500 to 2,000 new distributors—all of this happens online.

The landscape today differs substantially from when we started. Back then, Facebook was our primary social media platform, boasting a user base of 600 million. But as the digital world has grown and diversified, so have our strategies for growth and customer acquisition.

In the realm of branding and brand positioning, especially within the context of digital spaces and social media, there are vital steps you must take to ensure that your brand not only resonates with your target audience but also dominates their minds when considering solutions your brand provides.

Firstly, grab a pen and paper or your iPad with a stylus, and commit to writing down detailed information about your ideal customer. You need to understand your target market — the people most likely to need, want, and ultimately purchase your products or services.

Brand positioning refers to the process of carving a unique space in the minds of your potential customers, becoming the go-to solution for a specific need or desire. The goal is for your brand to be the first that comes to mind when customers think about a particular product or service.

Consider Tesla, for instance. Today, when people think about electric cars, Tesla immediately springs to mind. Despite numerous other companies in this market, Tesla`s brand positioning is so robust that it holds a commanding presence in the consumer`s mind.

Another excellent example of strong brand positioning is Red Bull. When energy drinks are the topic, Red Bull usually dominates the conversation. These brands demonstrate the power of brand positioning, though the process is often different for larger corporations compared to smaller businesses or individual entrepreneurs. Nevertheless, the underlying principles remain the same.

When it comes to developing your brand, it`s vital to keep things simple, particularly in the initial stages. As a small business or individual entrepreneur, you may not have the resources to aim for a brand recognition level like Apple, Tesla, or Coca-Cola. Instead, your goal should be to become a recognizable entity, a go-to person within your particular niche. You may not be the first to come to mind, but with the right branding, you can become a significant player.

The initial step in this journey is to define your ideal customer clearly. Imagine them, give them a name, say, Maria or John, depending on whether your product is designed more for men or women. Make no mistake, the phrase "my product is for everybody" is misleading and not beneficial for effective brand positioning. You must narrow down your audience to establish a strong brand.

Consider the age of your ideal customer. What city, country, or region do they live in? These details are critical if your business has geolocation restrictions or can only serve customers who speak a certain language. For instance, if you`re targeting Italian speakers and can only serve in Italy, your branding strategy must reflect this. Your branding strategy will be entirely different if your target customers speak English. Understanding these key details about your ideal customer is a fundamental step in successful brand positioning.

In our journey of brand positioning, we now arrive at an important crossroads where we must delve deeper into understanding our ideal customer beyond just the demographics. While the customer`s gender, age, language, and geographical location provide a general outline, it`s equally important, if not more, to delve into the psychographics — their needs, wants, pains, frustrations, and emotional connections.

Ask yourself, what is my customer`s primary problem or pain point? What are their frustrations? Are there specific emotions linked to this problem? Understanding this emotional landscape can lead to more effective communication strategies and greater customer engagement.

Next, consider the common objections your customer might have concerning your solution. This isn`t limited to objections about the product itself but any potential obstacles they perceive towards the solution they seek. For instance, if you`re selling a nutritional product, such as a weight loss shake, what might hold them back? It could be concerned about taste, cost, time commitment, or doubts about its effectiveness.

Moreover, you need to identify your customers` goals and dreams. What are they hoping to achieve or gain by seeking out your product or service?

Once you`ve compiled all this information, from demographic data to emotional connections to objections, you will have a comprehensive profile of your ideal customer. It is a powerful tool in your arsenal.

For instance, you might come up with a profile like "Maria, a 35-year-old Italian woman who struggles with maintaining a healthy weight due to her busy lifestyle. She is skeptical about nutritional shakes, worrying about their taste and ability to satiate her. Her ultimate goal is achieving a healthy body weight and feeling confident in her skin."

Coach's Notes: Creating a detailed customer persona like "Maria" is vital in understanding your audience. This depth of understanding helps tailor your marketing strategy and establish a robust brand. What can you do to help you understand your customer better?

This level of detail in understanding your customers will be instrumental in your brand positioning efforts.

In our process of understanding our ideal customer, it's crucial to be specific and precise. Let's take weight loss as an example. It isn't enough to broadly classify your customer's problem as "weight loss." You need to delve deeper. How many kilos does your customer want to lose specifically? It could be between three to five kilograms.

Likewise, their frustrations need to be clearly identified. They might feel uncomfortable when going to the beach, perhaps due to feelings of self-consciousness about their body. They might feel frustration when they don't receive the attention they want from the opposite sex, or they might experience embarrassment when shopping for clothes and not fitting into the sizes they desire.

The emotions attached to these frustrations can be feelings of disappointment, embarrassment, or a lack of self-esteem. By contrast, their dream might be to regain a sense of confidence and love for themselves. They might fantasize about feeling relaxed and proud when they see their reflection in the mirror or aspire to comfortably wear their desired clothing sizes.

This level of specificity needs to be applied across different industries. For example, the customer's problem in skincare isn't merely "wanting better skin." It's much more detailed than that. They may want to reduce the visibility of certain skin blemishes or achieve a certain level of skin glow.

Creating these detailed customer profiles allows for a deeper understanding of your target audience, leading to more effective brand positioning and marketing strategies.

The essence of truly understanding your customers lies in the specifics. I encourage you to delve deeply into their lives when you imagine your interactions with them. For example, if you`re selling skincare products, your customer might feel self-conscious during social outings, always trying to hide their face during photos and avoiding selfies. Explore these scenarios and emotions to create a detailed list of potential customer problems, frustrations, objections, goals, and dreams.

Now, let`s delve into a real-world example from two people in my team. This is crucial because it demonstrates the power of specificity. I have two women from my Spanish team: Luz and Alicia. Both are in their 50s, an age range typically seen as a hurdle when building a strong social media presence. But age did not deter them. Instead, they used it as an asset. They chose to focus exclusively on women experiencing menopause, a group with which they shared not only age but also personal experiences.

Their chosen demographic was women aged 45 and above grappling with the symptoms and side effects of menopause - from the hot flashes that make you throw open your windows in the middle of the night to the emotional rollercoaster that comes with hormonal changes.

In creating this specific avatar, their customer profile, they started with their stories and experiences. Luz and Alicia had used our products and seen a significant improvement in managing their menopausal symptoms. Their love for the products stemmed from personal success, providing them with a powerful foundation from which to build their business. It wasn`t just about selling products; they were offering solutions to problems they had once faced. That`s why their strategy works.

Despite starting from scratch on social media, they rapidly gained traction and amassed tens of thousands of followers. Alicia, for instance, has over 100,000 followers on TikTok, while Luz saw her followership explode from 20,000 to 80,000 in just a week. This growth wasn`t by accident; it was a result of a well-executed strategy.

Over a span of three to four weeks, they witnessed an incredible surge in their followers on Instagram and TikTok, reaching close to 100,000 followers on each platform. What led to this astounding growth? Their pinpointed focus. They weren`t trying to sell their products to everyone. Their target was explicit: women dealing with menopause and the associated symptoms, whether it`s hot flashes disrupting their nights or other physical changes caused by this transition. They took the time to detail all these symptoms and created a targeted solution, which we`ll delve into next.

It is important to truly understand your audience`s issues, including their physical, emotional, and social challenges. For instance, women experiencing menopause may grapple with mood swings that affect their social interactions. Similarly, individuals seeking to lose weight may feel self-conscious about their appearance and avoid social gatherings.

Once you`ve compiled a comprehensive list of these challenges, it`s time to craft content that directly addresses these pain points. This is precisely what our case study subjects, Luz and Alicia, did. They painstakingly created a list that detailed the various struggles associated with menopause – from sleep disturbances to unexplained weight gain and even the occasional tendency to respond harshly to loved ones.

Armed with this information, they set about producing content that resonated with their target audience – women in their menopause stage who faced similar issues. Their content delved into topics such as how to manage sleepless nights or cope with weight gain during menopause, and they even touched on managing mood swings to maintain harmonious relationships. By doing so, they were able to establish a direct connection with their ideal customers, resulting in significant success for their brand.

Let`s look at a couple more examples from people on my team. Elisa from Italy and Imani from Morocco have successfully utilized the system we`ve discussed, but their approaches are quite distinct, demonstrating the system`s versatility.

Elisa, for instance, is well-known for her personalized approach. She recognizes that young women have struggles of their own and focuses on supporting young women with weight loss, cellulite, and hydric retention symptoms. To address this, she offers a solution to her audience that has helped her navigate these challenges. She effectively creates a strong connection with her potential customers by sharing her personal journey and the solutions she has discovered.

Then there`s Imani, who employs a different but equally effective strategy. Imani comes from a place where the belief that it is hard to connect with the outside world is very prevalent. Many people think they cannot build a business because they don`t speak the language or are not working in an open country for their company. Imane built a business from scratch, and she got 100,000 followers on Instagram, all by focusing on women who speak her language, speaking to Arabian and Moroccan Women. She helped them to be in shape, stay healthy and make money to be independent. She knows her target and speaks directly to the problem of women like her living as an expat. With a keen understanding of her ideal customer, Imani creates content that resonates deeply with her target audience. She addresses the pain points and helps empower women from her native area.

Both strategies are highly effective in their own way. While Elisa`s strategy might result in fewer sales, she is able to build a stronger and more loyal customer base. On the other hand, Imani`s approach may lead to higher sales but might require continuous effort to maintain customer interest and loyalty.

Let`s examine Elisa`s strategy, which centers on her personal journey and transformation. Elisa has established her brand positioning by aligning it with her own story, and this personal touch has made her brand relatable and appealing to a specific demographic.

Elisa targets primarily younger women, roughly between the ages of 25 and 35. Her story of weight loss, overcoming health issues, and general self-improvement resonates deeply with this audience. As such, she crafts her content to reflect this journey, often sharing testimonials, success stories, and her personal experiences.

In particular, she consistently publishes similar types of content. The reasoning behind this approach is that by sharing relatable content, she forms a connection with her potential customers, thus effectively marketing her brand. This includes discussing the benefits of being in good shape, sharing her workouts, and talking about the positive changes she has experienced.

While she occasionally addresses the needs of other groups, like mothers, her primary focus remains on younger women. Despite having the potential to appeal to a broader demographic, Elisa chooses to specialize in one area, making her brand more recognizable and compelling to her target audience.

Elisa`s strategic branding revolves around her personal transformation and the benefits she gained from it, a story that resonates deeply with her target demographic. She ensures a strong and lasting connection with her audience by being consistent in the content she shares. This example demonstrates how understanding your audience and personalizing your brand accordingly can lead to a successful business.

Imani, who hails from Morocco. Imani is not only one of the top sellers on the team but also one of the most successful recruiters. Interestingly, Morocco is not a market directly serviced by my company, so Imani has had to devise a unique strategy.

Imani recognized the potential of connecting with women who share her cultural and linguistic background. Therefore, she positions her brand to resonate with Moroccan women, particularly those living outside their home country. She communicates predominantly in Arabic, particularly the Moroccan dialect, to connect more deeply with her audience.

Her focus is on addressing the unique challenges faced by these women. Often, these challenges stem from cultural or religious norms that might restrict their opportunities or influence their lifestyle choices. Imani tailors her messages to speak directly to these women, empathizing with their struggles and offering solutions that fit within their specific context.

By identifying this niche, Imani amplifies her message and creates a strong sense of community and belonging among her audience. In doing so, she has effectively turned a potential limitation, the fact that our company doesn`t ship to Morocco, into a unique selling point. This demonstrates the power of brand positioning and understanding the specific needs of your target audience.

Imani`s unique approach tailors her brand to speak directly to those women who feel out of place, stuck in their lives, perhaps having left their home countries in search of better opportunities only to find themselves unemployed and feeling helpless. This deep understanding of her target audience`s problems allows Imani to provide them with not only a product but also a solution.

Imani`s target audience is predominantly Arabic-speaking women from Morocco and Northern Africa, regardless of where they currently reside. This approach has allowed her to successfully expand her business in Italy, Eastern Europe, Spain, and Germany, all while remaining committed to serving the same demographic.

In essence, the key takeaway from this part of our journey is the importance of knowing your ideal customer, your avatar. It's not just about having a list of desired qualities in your customers but truly understanding their needs, their struggles, and their dreams. It's this deep understanding that will enable you to create a brand that genuinely resonates with your target market and provides solutions that are truly meaningful to them.

Through the examples and case studies we discussed, we learned about people who have successfully built enormous followings and have achieved robust weekly sales. Their secret weapon? They focused on understanding their ideal customer first and then developing consistent content that addresses that customer's needs, pain points, and desires.

The second step in this strategy involves creating content related to the attributes and characteristics you have outlined about your ideal customer. This content should be generated consistently every day, regardless of whether you feel you're repeating yourself. Remember that marketing thrives on repetition. A message doesn't truly penetrate until it has been heard numerous times.

Consider your brand as armor. Each piece is repeatedly forged and struck until it's strong and resilient. Each time you communicate your brand's story, it's like striking that piece of armor, reinforcing it until it's robust enough to withstand any challenge. So don't be hesitant to reinforce your brand's message continuously – it's an essential process in strengthening and solidifying your brand's identity.

Branding and marketing are iterative processes that require repeating the same content and actions consistently. As such, don't be shy about sharing the same content, and don't hesitate to create content daily.

This repetition ensures that your brand`s message is seen and heard, solidifying it in the minds of your audience.

Moreover, it`s crucial to include a call to action in your content. While you may not need to include it in every piece of content, it should be a common occurrence. Calls to action are essential because they invite your audience to engage with you and initiate a conversation.

Once a conversation has begun, it`s time to delve deeper. I would love to expand on this topic in this chapter, but time and space may not permit. However, I`ll briefly mention that when you`re in a conversation with a potential customer, it`s crucial to create a deep connection. This interaction usually involves a five-step approach:

1. Initiate the connection.

2. Confirm if the individual aligns with your ideal customer profile.

3. Inquire about their reasons for reaching out to you.

4. Discover why they`ve shown interest.

5. Understand why they decided to engage with your content, whether by filling out a form or commenting on your posts.

This process is not only about attracting the right people, but also about ensuring that your approach aligns with their needs and interests. The goal is to understand their motivations, which will enable you to serve them better.

In the next step of the process, qualifying your prospects becomes essential. It involves asking them questions related to their problems, the solutions they`ve tried in the past, and the dreams and goals they harbor. As you delve into these three areas, you`ll effectively gauge whether the prospect is a good fit for your offerings.

Maintaining a connection with your prospects is equally important. Employ the "Feel, Felt, Found" strategy; Acknowledge that you understand their situation, explain that you or someone else felt the same way, and share how a solution was found. Testimonials can also serve as powerful tools in bolstering your credibility.

After qualifying the prospect and fostering a connection, it`s time to present your product or service and move towards closing the sale. If the prospect doesn`t convert immediately, it`s important to follow up.

Sales negotiation is a vital component in attracting customers, as much as brand positioning, creating an ideal customer profile, and producing and publishing daily content are. Remember, repetition is key and should not be feared.

Coach's Notes: Imagine your brand like a suit of armor - it gets stronger every time you share your story. Don't shy away from repeating your message or making regular calls to action. Make friends with your customers, and get to know their likes and dreams. This will help you give them what they need. Always stay in touch and present your stuff in an irresistible way. If they don't bite at first, just follow up! Remember, your brand becomes ironclad through constant chit-chat and repetition. Keep it up!

"She Let God set a table for her, that was her turning point."

— Tiffini, House of Belonging

SUE JONES

- One of the founding leaders within the largest organization at company

- Recognized in 2023 as one of the top 25 in the company.

- Leads a very large team of top performers with love, compassion, and humility.

- Maintains the highest sales levels while also consistently maintaining one of the highest ranks within the compensation plan.

- Multiple Incentive Trip Earner.

- Sue is married with 7 children and 7 grandchildren.

The Fortune is in the Follow-Up; How to get More Sales, Referrals, and Team Members by Taking Good Care of Your Customers

I was first exposed to Network Marketing at the tender age of 19. At the time, I had no clue what Network Marketing was or that you could make a career and earn an income from the profession. In all actuality, only a select few made it to the top, and everyone else was just along for the ride. I dabbled in a few different companies over the years, spending more than I was making, and it wasn`t until 2020 and a partnership with my current company that I realized true success and replaced the income from my 9-5 corporate job. Now remember that 2020 was the beginning of a global pandemic, and honestly, I thought it was the worst possible time to start a new business, but I trusted the women paving the way with this new company and knew in my gut that they were onto something big. Just thirty days into my new business, I hit the leadership level of the company and have maintained or exceeded that level ever since.

There is something to say about follow-up and the power of suggestion and how this can be an effective tool in your business to sell more products, sponsor more teammates, and nurture your relationships, both with your clients and team. If you have been in this industry for any length of the time you have undoubtedly heard the phrase, "The fortune is in the follow-up," but what is the power of suggestion, and how does it relate to your network marketing business and relationships in general?

Coach's Notes: In this chapter, Sue emphasizes the importance of follow-up in the network marketing profession. She shares her personal journey, starting from the age of 19, and how she finally found true success in 2020 with her current company. Sue's message resonates with the idea that "the fortune is in the follow-up." By taking care of customers, nurturing relationships, and providing value, you can achieve more sales and referrals and build a strong team. Remember, consistent follow-up shows your customers that you care and appreciate them, leading to long-term success and loyalty.

The power of suggestion is when an individual has an idea conveyed to them, and that idea, in turn, becomes a reality, sounds simple, right?

In psychology, this is how psychologists help a patient modify their behavior. If a person believes in an expected outcome, they are more likely to achieve that outcome automatically. We can best relate to this when you are asked to visualize yourself as the rank you want to be or imagine yourself on an incentive trip you're trying to earn. That belief will propel your thoughts into action, and actions will keep the momentum moving forward in your business.

Another way to use the power of suggestion is by thinking bigger and broader when it comes to your clients. For example, let's say a prospect contacted you and said they wanted a product you offer. You could honor their request and sell them the product, and they'd be on their merry way OR, you could ask them some questions like - what issue are they trying to correct? Have they been using something to help with this issue already? What else do they use, and do they have a regular routine? By taking the time to have a conversation with your prospect/customer, you will be prompted by ways to help them with their concerns; they will know you care about them more than just making the sale. If you can develop a good understanding of your customer's needs and pain points, you will build trust and enhance your customer relationships. Make suggestions and be a problem solver! When you solve problems, you will be more likely to retain clients over the long term. It shows your customers that you're willing to put time into understanding their concerns. In doing so, you're proving you value them, and in a competitive market, this will make you stand out. When they feel appreciated, they'll be more likely to be loyal to your brand and to you. Remember, a satisfied customer is the best source of promoting your business and acquiring new customers because when customers are happy, they will refer their friends and family to you. The ultimate goal is to build trust, confidence, and belief; belief in you, your product, and your company!

Coach's Notes: Sue delves into the psychology of the power of suggestion and how it can positively impact your network marketing business. You can propel your thoughts into action by believing in the outcomes you desire and visualizing your success. She shares practical ways to use the power of suggestion with your clients, guiding them towards solutions that meet their needs. Being attentive, problem-solving, and building trust through follow-up will retain customers and lead to happy referrals. Embrace the power of suggestion to transform your business.

You might be asking, "What is the big deal," and why is follow-up important?

First and foremost, follow-up is about connections. In the Network Marketing profession, following up is one of the most important skills you need to master. If you don`t follow up, the conversation is over. Strong relationships in business and in life are formed over time across multiple interactions. Following up is a way to build and maintain relationships, show appreciation, and demonstrate your interest in more than just a sales transaction. It is the ultimate sign that you don`t take your customers for granted. Follow-ups can benefit your business, help improve communication between you and your customers, and build trust. Following up with customers is a type of marketing and can be a valuable asset when growing your business.

Customers will feel more valued when you follow up with them. You must remember that not all potential customers are ready to buy the first time you have contact with them. This is where relationship building comes into play because the more communication that has transpired, the more likely, you will be thought of when the customer needs a product like yours, and the fact that you have been in touch on a regular basis will matter.

Make sure your customer is happy and satisfied. You have to work on customer retention; follow-up is a large part of that. An unhappy customer will, more often than not, switch to a competitor rather than complain directly to you. Address any issues or concerns BEFORE they become a problem.

Follow-up gives you an opportunity for feedback and to learn if there are any problems with your product or service. You will also explore whether there are any unmet needs you may have a solution for. Follow-up is an act of service to show you care – have you ever purchased a product or service and then felt ghosted by the person who helped you? it`s not a good feeling and doesn`t make you want to do business with that person in the future. Don`t get me wrong, there is no "expectation," but being a good human and saying "thank you"; for supporting your business can go a long way! It`s the personal touch that counts!

Repeat business – you have a better chance of having repeat business when you follow up with your customer and improve customer retention. A happy customer will consider doing business with you in the future, and keeping in touch is a great way to upsell or make a new sale.

Happy customers refer their friends and family, which helps sustain your business long term. When you follow up, you are an example for prospective teammates. When a customer decides to join your team, you have initiated training on how you take care of them as a customer.

Implement your own follow-up system to convert a higher number of prospects - this goes beyond customers and translates to the way you keep track of people you have talked to about the opportunity. How often do you check in with them? Have their circumstances changed since the last time you talked? If you have made a genuine connection, you will know what`s happening in their lives and when it is appropriate to reach out to them in the future.

By not following up with prospects and/or customers, you put your reputation at risk and force them to take their business elsewhere.

Ways to Follow-up and Ideas for Good Customer Service

I am proud to say that I learned my customer service skills from my work experience at Nordstrom. It`s no secret that the Nordstrom company is known for its stellar customer service, and its reputation was built on this simple yet effective principle. I remember often hearing "the customer is always right," whether you believe that or not, your attitude around this concept will be a factor in your business success.

There are many ways to follow up, and most, if not all of those tools are already at our disposal. Not only do we have email and text, but we often forget that initiating a phone call and having your client hear your voice can go a long way. One of my favorite tools is to send a handwritten note or thank you card in the mail. A personal note in the mail is a nice surprise and can bring joy to the recipient.

If a customer has purchased a product from you, there are stages throughout the transaction where follow-up would be appropriate.

Some of those stages include:

- Acknowledge that you received their order and send a thank you note.

- Let your customer know when their order has shipped and/or is scheduled to arrive.

- Provide instruction on products and their use, if applicable.

- Contact your client a week after their products have arrived to check in and see how it`s going, and if they have any questions.

- Put your customers and prospects on a follow-up schedule and use a contact management system if necessary to make sure your contact remains consistent.

- Send general greetings like Happy Birthday and Merry Christmas etc.

- Practice gratitude and send notes of thanks and appreciation.

- Text, phone, or messenger – the important thing is not so much the "how," but that you follow up!

The key to effective follow-up is to make each interaction value-added. If the only time you follow up with a client and prospect is to try to get something from them or try and get them to buy from you, they will soon try to avoid you and dread your messages. So instead of only following up to ask for something, try to follow up in ways that they find useful. When you provide value, they`ll actually look forward to hearing from you.

The "value" that you provide in the communication with your customers and teammates depends on the type of business you have but could be things like a product tip, helpful information you`ve discovered, or suggestions based on the season. Be focused on the activity of following up, and don`t get tied to the results. Be a good human, be kind, and care about the people you come in contact with; the rest will follow.

Sometimes people struggle to follow up out of fear. Fear of rejection, fear of being annoying or a bother, and fear of being salesy or spammy. The best way to get around these feelings is to change your mindset and view your contact as coming from a place of service. When you focus on serving and not being tied to the outcome, you will actually feel the freedom to connect without apprehension.

Create a Follow-up System that Works for you and your Business

Other than the instances mentioned above, I strive to follow up with my customers and team at least once a month. This follow-up would be in addition to things like sending a Birthday greeting, saying Merry Christmas, or simply a note of gratitude for being in my life and being a friend. I believe that when you make someone feel special or appreciated, they will feel that the connection is genuine and heartfelt. The key to converting a higher number of prospects lies in how well you have managed to connect and build a relationship. People want to do business and be in business with someone they can trust and someone they like. Just because you`ve asked once and your customer or prospect said no, that just means "no, not right now." Circumstances change, and you never know when the timing may be right. Remember to always ask the question... if you don`t ask, the answer is always no!

Coach's Notes: Sue highlights the value of effective follow-up as a crucial skill in the network marketing profession. Following up is about building and maintaining relationships, showing appreciation, and going beyond sales transactions. It's a key marketing tool that enhances communication and fosters trust with customers. You can establish genuine connections by creating a follow-up system tailored to your business, providing value-added interactions, and focusing on service rather than the outcome. Remember, follow-up is an ongoing process, and it's essential to be persistent, caring, and authentic to achieve success in this industry.

"Perfection is not attainable, but if we chase perfection we can catch excellence."

— Vince Lombardi

SUE LIBERATORE

- Earned three consecutive corporate trips.

- Reached levels in my company of Director 3 and Platinum 3 which means that I am building both a team and a customer base that has allowed me to earn more money than I have in my previous careers in Corporate Insurance and as a Co-Owner of a brick and mortar flower shop.

- I earned more in this company while fulfilling my passions in a year than I did in 4 years in my previous network marketing company, which shows that being authentically you makes a huge difference.

After the fall on the dog food can that shattered my bones, I never could have anticipated how drastically my life would change. The five orthopedic surgeries left me physically and emotionally drained, but I did not know this series of events would eventually lead me to a new path.

Once the surgeries were over, my body exhausted from the grueling recovery process, I looked forward to getting back to my passion - running a flower shop. It had always been my dream, and I had co-owned the shop for years. However, the neurologist shattered my hopes when he informed me that the job`s physical demands were no longer feasible.

Devastated, I was left wondering what to do next. How could I find something that would allow me to continue my recovery while pursuing a fulfilling career? During this dark period, I stumbled upon network marketing - an industry known for its flexibility and entrepreneurial opportunities.

I joined a health and wellness company, hoping that their products could aid in my ongoing recovery. With perseverance and dedication, I successfully promoted their range of health supplements. The flexibility of network marketing allowed me to work on my terms, something that traditional employment could never have offered me in my current condition.

Coach's Notes: Here's a great example of Sue showcasing her resilience and adaptability. Despite life's unexpected setbacks, she found a new passion that resonated with her. Try to draw on your own experiences and passions in your marketing journey. Embrace change and let it lead you to new, exciting opportunities!

However, as life often does, the company`s business model experienced a significant change. It didn`t align with my vision and aspirations anymore, so I made the difficult decision to switch to another network marketing company. This transition brought about unexpected dividends.

To my delight, the new company impressed me with its range of products, particularly a patented liquid collagen formulation designed specifically for horses, dogs, and cats. This discovery resonated deeply with me as an animal lover passionate about their well-being. Intrigued, I decided to give the human version of the product a try.

I initially began taking the product myself, hoping it would aid in my continued recovery. Astonishingly, I started experiencing positive results in the areas where I had undergone multiple surgeries. Encouraged by this newfound wellness, I decided to share the product with one of my beloved dogs, who had also faced her own health struggles.

To my amazement, it had a transformative effect on her. She regained her vitality, and her overall health drastically improved. It was an eye-opening experience that ignited a fire within me. I knew then that I had stumbled upon something remarkable that could truly make a difference in the lives of animals and their owners.

Despite the lack of emphasis on the animal product line within my upline, I immersed myself in learning everything I could about horses, dogs, and their specific needs and challenges. I studied the intricacies of animals that competed in various events, identifying the issues that hindered their peak performance and recovery. I was determined to help owners and their beloved animals look and feel their best.

Word quickly spread of my dedication and passion, and my network marketing business gradually evolved into a niche market focused on supporting the well-being of dogs and horses. I began collaborating with veterinarians, trainers, and fellow animal enthusiasts to create a supportive community that strived for these incredible creatures optimal health and peak performance.

Coach's Notes: This is where Sue's passion and authenticity shine through. She's deeply involved in learning about her target audience, in this case, animals and their needs. This level of commitment fosters trust and respect in your market. Always be learning folks, and let your passion guide your journey!

Little did I know that this unexpected discovery of a product would become the catalyst for a new chapter in my life. In the face of adversity, I found a calling that resonated with both my own recovery journey and my lifelong love for animals. Together, we would embark on a journey to improve their lives and create a lasting impact in the world of animals and their dedicated owners.

Seeing how my passion for the animal world has led to helping other animal lovers and helped grow my business has been incredible. This is truly what network marketing is all about. Building relationships is one of the biggest parts of this business, earning people`s trust. This is vital for success. This is particularly true when dealing with dog and horse owners, who often hold a deep bond and sense of responsibility towards their beloved animals.

For these individuals, their pets` well-being is of utmost importance, and they seek trustworthy and reliable products or services. By establishing genuine connections and demonstrating a sincere understanding of their needs and concerns, network marketers can gain the trust of dog and horse owners. This can be achieved through active listening, providing accurate information, and offering personalized solutions that cater to their specific requirements. Building trust takes time and effort, but once earned, it becomes the foundation for long-term relationships, repeat business and referrals. In this chapter, I want to cover how you can create long-lasting relationships that can, in turn, help your business.

In the dynamic world of network marketing, building genuine relationships and earning people`s trust are crucial steps toward long-term success. Recognizing the profound bond between pet owners and their beloved animals is essential for network marketers targeting the dog and horse community. These passionate individuals prioritize their pets` well-being and seek trustworthy products and services. To forge meaningful connections in this niche, network marketers must demonstrate a sincere understanding of their audience`s needs and concerns. This chapter explores how network marketers can leverage their own hobbies and interests to build relationships, foster trust, and create a lasting impact within the dog and horse community.

Authenticity and Shared Passion

Authenticity is the cornerstone of building meaningful relationships when connecting with the dog and horse community. As a network marketer, tapping into your own passion for animals can create an instant bond with potential customers. Your love for pets becomes a powerful driving force that infuses your interactions with genuine enthusiasm and warmth. Sharing personal stories and experiences related to your beloved pets humanizes you and establishes a common ground with pet owners. This personal touch fosters a sense of relatability, making your brand more approachable and trustworthy.

Your passion becomes contagious as you express genuine enthusiasm for your products or services. Pet owners often hold deep emotional connections with their animals and are naturally drawn to others who share their love for furry companions. By showcasing your shared passion for animals, you demonstrate your understanding of the pet owner`s world, and this authenticity resonates deeply within the dog and horse community. The sense of camaraderie you cultivate through your passion bridges the gap between you and potential customers, easing any initial reservations they might have about engaging with a network marketer.

Beyond establishing credibility and trust, your authentic approach lays the groundwork for long-lasting relationships with pet owners. When people sense that your interest in their well-being extends beyond business transactions, they are more likely to view you as a trusted advisor rather than just a salesperson. This sense of trust empowers pet owners to make informed decisions, confident that you genuinely have their best interests at heart. As a result, they are more receptive to your offerings and recommendations, fostering more organic and sustainable business growth within the dog and horse community.

Authenticity is the foundation of successful relationships within the dog and horse community in network marketing. Your passion for animals becomes a powerful connector, creating an instant bond with potential customers. By sharing personal stories and expressing genuine enthusiasm for your products or services, you establish credibility and trust among fellow pet owners. This authentic approach sets the stage for long-term connections, where pet owners perceive you as a trusted partner who genuinely cares about their well-being. As you embrace your love for animals in your network marketing endeavors, you`ll find that it becomes a driving force in creating enduring relationships and propelling your business to new heights within this passionate community.

Leveraging Social Media Platforms

In today`s digital age, social media has emerged as a powerful tool for community engagement, and for network marketers targeting the dog and horse community, it offers an invaluable platform to connect with potential customers. Facebook groups and Instagram communities dedicated to dogs and horses serve as virtual hubs where passionate pet owners congregate to share experiences and seek advice. As a network marketer, joining these relevant groups opens the door to building authentic relationships with fellow animal enthusiasts.

Active participation is key to establishing yourself as a reliable and knowledgeable resource within these social media communities. Engaging in discussions, offering meaningful insights, and providing helpful advice showcase your expertise and genuine interest in the concerns of pet owners. Consistently providing valuable content demonstrates your commitment to adding value to the community and positions you as a trustworthy figure.

Responding to queries with thoughtfulness and attentiveness further strengthens your reputation as a dependable source of information. As you engage with pet owners on social media, a sense of familiarity and trust naturally develops. This familiarity creates a connection that makes potential customers more likely to seek your products or services when the need arises. Building trust through consistent and genuine engagement on social media lays the foundation for enduring relationships.

Leveraging social media platforms such as Facebook groups and Instagram is highly effective in building relationships and earning people's trust. You establish credibility and authenticity by participating actively, providing valuable content, and engaging with pet owners in meaningful discussions. Responding to inquiries with expertise and attentiveness fosters trust over time, making potential customers more inclined to rely on you as a reliable resource for their pet-related needs. Embrace the power of social media engagement to cultivate lasting connections, solidify your position as a trusted advisor, and pave the way for meaningful interactions with the passionate dog and horse community.

In-Person Engagement

While social media serves as an excellent platform to begin building connections, the power of face-to-face interactions should always be considered. To foster lasting relationships, consider attending dog shows, horse events, and other relevant gatherings where you can engage directly with pet owners. These events provide an ideal setting to connect with like-minded individuals who share your passion for animals. Approach conversations with a genuine interest in their passions and concerns, and let your love for pets shine through your interactions.

When engaging in face-to-face conversations, actively listen to pet owners' needs, challenges, and goals. Take the time to understand their specific concerns, whether finding the perfect nutrition for their four-legged companions or seeking effective training techniques. Demonstrating genuine empathy and concern creates a sense of trust and rapport that forms the foundation for meaningful relationships. These personal touch points solidify your credibility and showcase your commitment to the well-being of beloved animals, making you a reliable and caring resource within the community.

At dog and horse events, seize the opportunity to engage in meaningful conversations with pet owners. Initiate discussions, ask questions, and be attentive to their responses. As you listen attentively to their needs and challenges, you gain invaluable insights that will allow you to tailor your solutions better to serve them effectively. Demonstrating this level of attentiveness shows your dedication to understanding their unique circumstances and elevates your position as a trusted advisor who genuinely cares about their pet's health and happiness.

In-person interactions provide an excellent platform to showcase your expertise and product knowledge. Offer valuable insights and advice, guiding pet owners toward the best choices for their animal companions. By providing solutions that cater to their individual requirements, you establish yourself as a reliable resource and build a sense of dependability that extends far beyond the initial interaction.

While social media serves as an essential starting point in building relationships with the dog and horse community, the significance of face-to-face interactions cannot be underestimated. Attending dog shows, horse events, and other relevant gatherings provides a unique opportunity to connect on a personal level, demonstrating your passion for animals and genuine interest in the concerns of pet owners. By actively listening to their needs and challenges and offering tailored solutions, you solidify your credibility and commitment to their beloved animal's well-being. Embrace the power of in-person engagement to foster long-lasting relationships, becoming a trusted advisor and reliable resource within the passionate dog and horse community.

Understanding Pet Owners' Well-being

The well-being of pet owners is intricately connected to that of their animals. Network marketers can demonstrate genuine care by recognizing the importance of self-care for these individuals. Offer products or services that cater to their personal well-being, such as health and wellness solutions or opportunities to supplement their income. By addressing their needs beyond the realm of pet care, you showcase your dedication to their overall happiness and success.

It is crucial for owners to recognize the importance of taking care of themselves in order to care for their animals. Whether it is maintaining good physical health or finding additional sources of income, understanding their priorities and providing solutions aligning with their biggest concerns can be a game-changer. By offering products or services that enhance their well-being or provide means for financial stability, you can demonstrate your dedication to their overall success and foster long-lasting relationships based on trust, support, and mutual growth.

Coach's Notes: Here, Sue emphasizes the importance of self-care for pet owners, not just the pets themselves. This empathetic approach shows her broader concern for her customer's well-being. Remember, caring about your customer's overall well-being, not just their immediate needs, helps in building long-lasting, meaningful relationships!

Honesty and Transparency

In network marketing, honesty, and transparency are not just moral imperatives; they are powerful tools for establishing credibility and building enduring relationships. By being forthright about the benefits and limitations of your products or services, you set realistic expectations for pet owners. Transparency creates an atmosphere of trust, where potential customers feel assured that they are making informed decisions. When you avoid making unrealistic promises and focus on accurate information, you position yourself as a reliable authority in the dog and horse community.

Emphasizing transparency in your interactions allows you to proactively address any concerns or doubts that pet owners may have. You demonstrate your commitment to their satisfaction and well-being by openly discussing potential drawbacks or challenges. Such authenticity creates an open dialogue with customers, fostering an environment where they feel comfortable voicing their questions or apprehensions. When pet owners recognize your integrity and genuine care for their best interests, they are more likely to view you as a trusted partner in their pet-related journey. This trust becomes the bedrock of lasting relationships, leading to repeat business and word-of-mouth referrals within the close-knit dog and horse community.

Conclusion

In the dog and horse community, building relationships and earning people`s trust are essential for success in network marketing. By leveraging your own passion for animals, engaging on social media platforms, participating in in-person events, understanding pet owners` well-being, and demonstrating honesty and transparency, you can create authentic connections that resonate with this passionate audience. Building lasting relationships in this niche leads to repeat business and fosters a supportive network of loyal customers who advocate for your brand. Embrace your hobbies as a network marketer, and watch as your genuine interest and dedication to the pet community pave the way to a thriving and rewarding business endeavor.

"Make it Make Sense."

– Tanisha Bowman

TANISHA BOWMAN

- Achieved a six-figure income.

- Enjoyed the privilege of winning seven all-expenses-paid trips, five of which were shared with my spouse.

- Experienced the thrill of being a part of a powerful panel, eliciting a standing ovation while inspiring others with the belief that anything is attainable.

- Graced the stage in Las Vegas on multiple occasions.

- Received numerous awards and gifts as a testament to my ranking in the top .1% of my company, and has had the honor of leading a rapidly expanding team of over 3,000 enthusiastic business partners.

Goals + Mindset = Success

My name is Tanisha L. Bowman, and I am a retired business owner, motivational speaker, certified empowerment coach, Co-Author, and founder of BrokeCan Coaching Services and BrokeCan INC.

Like most people, I started a business with direct sales to make a few extra dollars and receive a discount. Six years ago, I did not know how much money the business would bring me. I had no idea that I would retire from my J.O.B.; Just Over Broke. I had no idea I would meet and connect with so many amazing people and build many new relationships.

Direct Sales changed my life. It allowed me to discover my calling and walk into my gifts and talents as a motivational speaker and empowerment coach who loves to encourage and inspire others. My business plan was totally different from God`s plan, and His plan is always better.

My story of success is rare, but I know that if God did it for me, He could surely do it for you. So how did it happen to me? I learned the importance of setting goals early in my business, and I started focusing on defining a goal.

A goal in football, soccer, rugby, hockey (and some other games) is a pair of posts linked by a crossbar and often with a net attached behind it, forming a space into or over which the ball has to be sent in order to score. Believing in yourself is an important key to success. It doesn`t matter how much you read, train, or even work. If you don`t believe it, you will never see it. The definition of a goal caught my attention because it triggered my mindset. I would never make the goal if I did not change my mindset. The two bars outside of the goal were my negative beliefs about myself. Reaching my goal would become a challenge if I didn`t believe in myself.

To me, mindset is what you believe about yourself impacts your success or failure. I learned quickly that I would begin working like it if I truly believed I could succeed. I had several reasons not to believe in myself, and for many years the negative beliefs I believed about myself were because of my past failures and hurt. I grew up in the city of Detroit with my mom on drugs. I became a teenage mom at the age of fifteen and dropped out of high school at the age of sixteen. I gave up at an early age. I was afraid to set major goals and didn`t believe God`s beliefs about me. I`m telling you this because some of you are not moving in your business simply because you don`t believe it`s possible.

You are setting new goals for your business every year, and you don`t have your mindset on the goal. It`s time to start believing in who you are and whose you are; it`s time to stop playing small. I played small because I considered myself small in this huge world.

Coach's Notes: Tanisha brilliantly ties the concept of a sports goal to life ambitions, underscoring the importance of self-belief in achieving success. Her personal realization becomes a universal lesson - it's not just about reaching the goal, but the mindset that carries you there.

Five Ways to Help Change Your Mindset

1. Practice self-awareness: Begin by developing a greater understanding of your current mindset. Pay attention to your thoughts, beliefs, and emotions. Notice any negative or limiting patterns that may be holding you back. Change your language! Example I could recruit more team members but take "but" off, stop the sentence, and start writing down ways that you can gain more team members.

2. Challenge your beliefs: Examine your existing beliefs and question their validity. Ask yourself whether they are serving you positively or holding you back. Look for evidence that supports alternative perspectives or more empowering beliefs. Engage in critical thinking and open yourself up to new ideas and possibilities.

3. Surround yourself with positive influences: CHECK YOUR CIRCLE! This was huge for me! What you allow to come in is what will come out. The people you spend time with can greatly impact your mindset. Seek out individuals who have a positive and growth-oriented mindset. Surrounding yourself with supportive, optimistic, and motivated individuals who can inspire you and help reshape your own thinking.

4. Embrace failure and learn from it: Adopt a mindset that views failure as a learning opportunity rather than a negative outcome. The only way you fail is if you fail to try to succeed.

   Understand that setbacks and mistakes are a natural part of growth and development. Embrace them as valuable lessons that provide insight and propel you forward.

   Some of you are ready to start a business, but fear is holding you back. It`s been a goal of yours for the last five years, but you have yet to start. It`s because you haven`t shifted your mindset. I wish I knew the mindset fairy, and she could come in and wave a magic wand, and now you believe in yourself. If it were that simple, that`s the business I would invest in. Unfortunately, it`s not. It starts with a decision.

   I decided my dreams were just as important as the CEO I worked for. I decided that no matter how much I was making, I couldn`t make enough to give me my time back. My time is priceless, and eight hours a day at someone else`s dream would no longer be my nightmare. I`m not telling you this so you can immediately quit your job. I`m telling you this so you can start to invest the overtime in yourself, so you don`t have to work overtime forever.

Coach's Notes: Tanisha's concrete, actionable strategies for mindset change are an asset to any entrepreneur. Her emphasis on self-awareness and challenging beliefs can be the catalyst for personal transformation. Remember, your circle of influence is critical.

5. Practice positive self-talk and affirmations: Pay attention to your inner dialogue and replace negative self-talk with positive affirmations. Challenge self-limiting beliefs by consciously reframing them into positive and empowering statements. Regularly remind yourself of your strengths, capabilities, and potential for growth. Affirmations can help rewire your thinking patterns and reinforce a more positive and constructive mindset.

Here is a list of affirmations I say every day.

- I AM BEAUTIFUL.

- I AM BOLD.

- I AM GIFTED.

- I AM TALENTED.

- NO WEAPON FORMED AGAINST ME SHALL PROSPER.

- I CAN DO ALL THINGS THROUGH CHRIST, WHO STRENGTHENS ME.

- THIS IS THE DAY THE LORD HAS MADE; LET US REJOICE AND BE GLAD IN IT.

I keep it basic and simple. Depending on what is going on that day, I may add a few more, but I make sure to speak life over my life every day. If you don`t believe these things about yourself, how can you expect anyone else to believe them? I stand in the mirror, and I have a conversation with myself. This may be a little overboard for some, but my dreams are a little overboard for some.

My Advice to You is to Challenge Yourself

Challenge yourself to speak affirmations over yourself and your business every day.

Challenge yourself to change your circle.

Challenge yourself to step outside your comfort zone.

Challenge yourself to beat your best.

Challenge yourself to celebrate the small wins.

Challenge yourself to prepare for the big wins.

Challenge yourself to create generational wealth.

Challenge yourself to break generational curses.

Challenge yourself to decree and declare that you deserve it.

Coach's Notes: The power of Tanisha's daily affirmations is in their simplicity and authenticity. Her practice of speaking life over herself inspires us to do the same, proving that change begins within. Encourage yourself with your own affirmations.

*"Once you see results,
it becomes an addiction."*

— Unknown

TYRONICA STANFORD CARTER

- 7 Figure Earner.

- 133,000 in downline.

- 2nd highest rank in the company.

- Named 2023 Southern Crescent Women in Business Top Women of Influence.

- Featured in Sheen National Magazine May/June 2023 Edition.

Creating Personalized Habits of Success to Reach Your Goals

I am all about giving my team the tools and resources necessary to succeed; this chapter will be nothing short of the same. I am excited to share with you what you need to be successful in network marketing. But, I want to caution here at the beginning of my chapter. These resources are not a value menu where you get to pick and choose what you do. Every step of the process is necessary to see your desired results! So strap up! Let`s get started!

Quarterly I do 12-week challenges for my team. When we begin, I post and create excitement for my team that we are starting the challenge. The post gets so many comments, tags, and shares because the anticipation of being challenged is in the air. Then, the week`s first challenge is posted, "It`s time to book your first party!" That post is occasionally met with silence. No excitement, no check-in to say that they have booked a party. People say they are all in, but then they pick and choose what challenges they want to do. That is not how successful businesses work. That is the hard truth, but you can`t say I`m all in or ask for help if you aren`t actually all in.

If you are here, reading or listening to this book, you are committing to going all in on your business. That means you aren`t picking and choosing what sounds fun, easy, or what you feel like doing. You are saying, "Tyronica, I am ready for the five-course meal! Bring it on!" I am here to give you what you want if you can commit to that. So let`s dig in!

Coach's Notes: I'm excited to guide you through Tyronica's incredible wisdom about building personalized habits of success. Remember, this isn't a pick-and-choose situation - it's an all-in journey to reach our goals. Tyronica teaches us to commit fully and embrace the challenges without half-measures. It's like sitting down for a five-course meal, not just a quick snack. Let's step up, own our responsibilities, and dig into the feast of success that Tyronica has so wonderfully prepared for us!

The first thing you all need to know, your upline or leader is not in charge of taking on the responsibilities of you and your business. Their job is to give you the tools that you need to succeed.

Think about baking a cake. If you are watching a famous chef on tv make the cake. They can entertain you, maybe even give you some tips, but they can`t bake the cake for you. Same thing with any expert, upline, or mentor. They can give you the flour, the sugar, the salt, and anything else you need, but you have to bake your own cake. It`s true. You need to stop looking around, thinking someone else is in charge of baking. NO ONE is here to do it for you. You have to be in charge of your responsibilities. I always tell my team, "I didn`t sign up to bake for y`all. You have to do it yourself. I am simply the grocery store for the ingredients!"

Honesty is important to me. That`s why I don`t sugarcoat my words in this chapter. You have to know that there are so many wonderful tools and ingredients to build a successful business in network marketing, but no one else is responsible for building it but you.

Mistakes are acceptable. Failures happen. The one thing that is not acceptable is excuses. People come up with so many excuses and reasons as to why they aren`t showing up for themselves or their businesses. Your excuses are your safety. They are what is keeping you stuck in the safety of your life. You may not like your life, but you are willing to fight, argue, and make excuses! I have seen people who have never had a business before become very successful. They do it by saying, "I am doing this." They don`t hide behind excuses and pick and choose what they are doing. They go all in on becoming the creators of their success.

Let`s go back to the analogy of baking a cake. Anyone that has baked knows that the ingredients are important. There is a huge difference between baking a cake with ingredients you got at the gas station vs. using the finest ingredients from a local artisan farm. Your ingredients matter!

Just think about how you are approaching your daily methods of operations. Are you talking to ten people a day? Great, but what type of ingredients did you bring to that conversation? Are you enthused? Do they believe you really love what you`re doing? Did you listen? There is a HUGE difference between bringing your best and just doing it to get it done. People can see through the fake.

Also, as you bake that cake, you will want to make sure you put the ingredients in order. We all know the sugar and butter must be creamed together before adding the eggs. I can`t tell you how often I have watched people try to build their businesses using the wrong formula. As a former educator of fifteen years, I always like to tell my team; you must complete and master first grade before moving to second. Though we dream of that senior year, there`s a process, and it can take years of building, growing, and learning before we get there. The directions to build your business are not hard, but they must be followed, and you have to do each step.

Coach's Notes: Let's dive into Tyronica's fantastic cake-baking analogy! It's a perfect illustration of our roles in network marketing. Just like baking, you have all the ingredients for success, but it's on you to mix them and bake your own cake - your business. Tyronica reminds us to ditch the excuses and be the creators of our success. How are we approaching our daily tasks? Are we using the finest ingredients in our conversations? Remember, we have to follow the recipe step by step - it's a process. Let's get baking!"

Finally, you have to trust the process. Have you ever had a cake in the oven and then decided to take a peek to see how it was doing? If you have, you could collapse the cake. You have to trust the process. You must trust the process when given a challenge from your upline or company. Don`t try and gauge if it is successful three weeks in. You have to trust the process and continue doing what you are learning.

It`s easy to get caught up in the marketing of other systems and see people say that they built a successful business overnight using some crazy system that you need to invest in right now. Don`t buy into the glitz and glam of what seems like a successful system. Remember that some cakes you see on tv are styrofoam decorated with fake fondant. It`s the same with what you are shown as a "successful business" online. Yes, successful businesses exist, but they aren`t built overnight.

Some of you want to be at the top of the Empire State Building, but you don`t even have a foundation to build on. You can`t get to the top of something you haven`t built yet. You need a solid foundation. The foundation is built on creating consistent habits in your business.

So let`s talk about habits of success. Creating personalized habits of success to reach your goals for this year is a system I love implementing to my team. I want you to think of four or five goals you want to achieve this year. These goals should be focused around your business, and depending on where you are in your business, will help you set those goals. I love having my team come up with goals because our goals help us solidify our habits of success. Your goals shouldn`t be small! They should be your ultimate business goals. Most people think too small when they come up with goals because they don`t want to fail. Remember, failure is a great teacher. I recently heard someone say, You didn`t fail; you just found a way that didn`t work.

My personalized habits of success formula for network marketing is simple. You are going to come up with a four-week program of DMOs (Daily Method of Operations) along with actionable steps that you can do every week that are going to help you get closer to accomplishing your goals. For example, I may decide my week one looks like this:

Compliment twenty-five people. Give out sample products to three people. Personally, call those you have recruited. These would be my DMOs for week one because my personal ultimate goal in my business is to grow my team and my sales. Creating weekly habits such as these will move me closer to that goal through my consistency.

Next, I will create my week two actionable steps and then move on to weeks three and four. Each week should build upon one another to drive momentum and challenge you. Once the four weeks are done, I don`t have to reinvent a new system for the next month. I recycle those same four weeks and do it the following month. This sets you up to create sustainable success habits. You can create your own habits of success based on your goals.

Some of you may still be trying to decide what goals you should set. Let me help you out with somewhere to start. Here are at least three goals I would like each of you to write down. You should be recruiting three people every single month. That is your first goal. Can you do more? Absolutely! But you need a baseline to hold yourself accountable and to keep your team growing. Your second goal should be to rank advance within your company. I don`t know what rank you are at now, and it doesn`t matter. When we set our sights on the next rank, we tell ourselves that there is more to be built. Our minds will set out to try and figure out how to make that happen. As I was once told, be grateful, but don`t settle. So whether you are brand new or have been part of the industry for a long time, one of your goals should be to always go for that next rank advancement. The third goal I want you to set for yourself is to work on your business every single day for the next 90 days. Yes, you read that correctly. I want you to go to work. Too often, we sell the dream of time freedom. Yes, that is a luxury of this business, but it is closer to the top of the Empire State Building than at the foundation of it. As you start your business, you are going to have to put the time in for your business! Whether you have a full-time job or have five babies at home, those should be the reasons you decide to go even harder. You have the time to work your business every single day for the next ninety days. While still working full-time, I never referred to my business as my "hustle" or "side gig." I always called it my "other 9-5" because I knew that in order to be successful, I couldn`t give more time and energy into someone else`s dream more than I did my own! I had to be a good employee to myself also.

I am positive that if you do this, your business will transform in a quarter and that second goal of hitting your next rank will be closer than it was when you started.

So there are three goals all set for you! Now it`s up to you to come up with the fourth and fifth goals. As you set the recipe for success, you are going to see that your habits continue to become more consistent, and you will start to see the fruits of your labors.

I hear people say all the time, "I`m not sure what I should be doing in my business this week. I feel so lost." I`m going to let you in on the truth. I know exactly why you feel lost. It is because you don`t have clear goals. It really is that simple. If you don`t take the time to create and write down your goals and how you want your life to look, you are going to feel lost.

Can you imagine sitting down with a travel agent and having them ask you where you want to go. You sit there confused and say, "I`m not sure." I can tell you right now that a travel agent is of no use to you if you don`t know where you want to go and what you want to experience.

Think about what changes in that example if you walk into the travel agent and say, "I want to vacation to a place in the world that has winter zipline, skiing, and really great restaurants all within walking distance of my hotel." That is something that the travel agent can help you figure out and plan. If you have no idea where your destination is and no idea how to get there; you are going to be lost.

Your habits of success are what help you get to the destination. I am always telling my team "Don`t write down fluff stuff." What that means is that you need to make sure that your habits of success are actionable tasks and that you are not just manifesting or thinking good thoughts. You should be able to say this habit of success I wrote down for the week will be effective in me reaching this specific goal right here. Your habit of success should be something that you can say you did. If the action doesn`t get you closer to your goal, it`s fluff. If you say you need to print orders. Of course, you do, but that`s more of a task of your business than a habit of success. How does printing your orders actually help you reach a goal? It doesn`t that`s fluff. Get rid of the fluff and secure your goals through habits with a successful plan to get you where you want to be.

You can do this. You can be highly successful and build your own Empire State Building. But you have to be willing to work and be consistent. Hard work pays off. Keep being innovative and creating your habits and success. I always say those most successful in business are those who hit the ground running on day one. If you lack in that area, don`t worry. Let today be your Day 1!

Coach's Notes: Tyronica's insight is spot-on! Trusting the process and setting ambitious goals are key. Love her four-week DMO plan - it's a practical, powerful tool for sustained success. Remember, success isn't built overnight. It's a daily commitment. So, let's ditch the fluff, stay focused and make every day count. Ready to bake your success cake? Let today be your Day 1!

"Our greatest weakness
lies in giving up.
The most certain way
to succeed is always
to try just one more time."

— Thomas Edison

CONCLUSION

Congratulations! You`ve made it to the end of this incredible journey, where you have been given the privilege to peer into the minds of some of the most successful leaders in network marketing. Through each chapter, every author has generously shared their insights, strategies, and stories of personal triumph.

This book was intended to inspire you and equip you with actionable strategies for success. But here is where the real challenge begins: It`s time for action. Yes, you`ve absorbed a wealth of knowledge, but remember, knowledge without action is like a car without fuel. It has the potential to go anywhere, but it will never leave the garage.

Our aim was to provide consumption information and spark implementation motivation. It is not enough to simply read about the principles of success; it is in their application that success is born. So, ask yourself: What will be your first step? Which strategies resonated most with you? How can you put what you`ve learned into action today?

Challenge yourself to start now. Test these principles, strategies, and techniques in your own business. Success doesn't always come from grand gestures but consistent small steps forward. So, move forward with purpose and drive. Remember, the speed at which you achieve success is up to you.

Each chapter in this book has been written by an author who once stood where you stand now. They took their first steps, faced challenges, and grew. Now, it's your turn. There's no better time than the present to take action and make your own mark in the world of network marketing.

Invite you to join me in *The Game of Networking* Facebook group. This vibrant community is where we continue the conversation, answer questions, and share experiences. You will get the chance to connect with me directly and meet many of the authors from this book and countless other network marketers like you.

I am deeply grateful for your trust and commitment to learning. Compiling this treasure trove of wisdom from the network marketing industry's finest minds has been an honor. Remember, the journey doesn't stop here. This book, your notes, and our Facebook group are your ongoing resources for inspiration and guidance.

Your journey to success in network marketing is just beginning. Now, armed with knowledge, inspiration, and a community of supporters, it's time for action. It's time to step into your power and create the success you've always envisioned. I can't wait to see what you'll achieve.